Lina Keupper

Quisisana Hygienic Cook Book

Lina Keupper

Quisisana Hygienic Cook Book

ISBN/EAN: 9783744782906

Printed in Europe, USA, Canada, Australia, Japan

Cover: Foto ©Andreas Hilbeck / pixelio.de

More available books at **www.hansebooks.com**

Quisisana
Hygienic Cook Book.

BY

MISS LINA KEUPPER,

Secretary of Quisisana Sanitarium,

ASHEVILLE, N. C.

The French Broad Press, Asheville

PREFACE.

Since our hygienic cooking has from the opening of our Sanitarium called forth so many favorable comments from our guests, because of its wholesomness and palatableness, we decided to write a cook book containing most of the dishes used in our institution, hoping that it will meet the approval of all who use it.

Only a well nourished body can be healthy and strong, and in order to be well fed we ought to know what to eat and how to prepare it.

Every one knows that we need for the building up of the body certain quantities of albumen, fat, etc.; but too little attention is paid to the necessary minerals and it is of the greatest importance for the body to have the proper amount of these as well.

Why are so many sedentary people enæmic? Because their diet consists mostly of meat, grains and the legumes which are particularly poor in soda and lime; if to this diet a certain amount of vegetables and fruits were added, their blood and bones would grow healthier. For many it is sufficient to acquire a taste for vegetables, and even when they do have them they are in most cases unwholesome, being unhygienically prepared, so that they are robbed of most of their hygienic properties. In order to retain within the vegetables these properties they should never be washed in hot water, nor should the water in which they are cooked be poured off, for it contains in solution the strength-giving minerals of the vegtable; therefore vegetables should be cooked in a very little water or steamed.

Nachrsalz: Dr. Lahmann, of Germany, seeing the necessity of adding to certain vegetables the mineral salts they lack, discovered, after long and various experiments, a process by which to make a preparation from the mineral substances of plants, which he appropriately calls "Naehrsalz," or nourishing salt. It is particularly useful in our diet since we can with it make many of our dishes more wholesome and digestible. We add it to meats and to those vegetables which do not contain a sufficient amount of the necessary minerals. Naehrsalz not only aids digestion but improves the flavor of the food. It is to be added to a dish only shortly before serving it, and for a dishful of vegetables, Naehrsalz the size of a pea only is needed.

Labmann's Cocoa, we have found to be the best and purest cocoa. It is made from the finest selected cocoa beans, is chemically free from grease, and contains naehrsalz, which improves its flavor and makes it more easily digested.

Nutcoa, we use in our kitchen for frying, shortening, etc. It is a pure product of the cocoanut and is more easily digested than any other kind of fat.

Grape Juice, is the pure juice of the grape entirely free from alchohol and one of the most wholesome and nourishing beverages. We use it much in our sanitarium since we never under any circumstances use alchoholic drinks.

Lemon Spice is made thus: Grate off the yellow part of lemon peel, mix it up with a good deal of granulated sugar and put it in a glass jar. It keeps for years when tightly closed. More peel may be added at any time. It is to be used only in small quantities, as spices of all kinds make the blood impure; we therefore use very little even of salt.

We have tried to explain German dishes as clearly as possible and hope we have succeeded in doing so.

INDEX.

vii

MENUS.

BREAKFAST.

First Day :

Fresh fruit
Oatmeal with sugar, cream and milk
Boiled eggs
Rye bread
Wheat bread
Muffins
Honey
Caramel cereal-coffee or Dr. Lahmann's cocoa

Second Day :

Cooked fruit
Wheat hearts with sugar, cream and milk
Scrambled eggs
Toast
Honey
Same drink as first day

Third Day :

Fresh fruit
Grits with sugar, cream and milk
Poached eggs
Corn bread and honey
The same drinks as first day.

Fourth Day :

Cooked fruit
Hominy with sugar, cream and milk
Corn pancakes
Maple syrup
The same drinks

Fifth Day :

Fresh fruit
Ralston breakfast food
Eggs on toast
Honey
The same drinks

Sixth Day :

Cooked fruit
Indian meal
Corn muffins
Soft boiled eggs
Honey
The same drinks

Seventh Day :

Fresh fruit
Petit John
Toast
Scrambled eggs
Honey
The same drinks

ix

DINNERS.

JANUARY.

January 1st :

Canned fruit
Barley soup
Cauliflower, baked
Beef roast
Red cabbage with apples
Mashed potatoes
Celery salad
Puckler ice cream.
Bread and butter

January 2nd :

Fresh fruit
Carrots with parsley
Green beans
Veal chops
Irish and sweet potatoes
Lettuce
Tapioca pudding
Bread and butter

January 3rd :

Cooked fruit
Cabbage
Dried peas with fried onion gravy
Mutton roast
Fried Irish potatoes.
Baked sweet potatoes
Celery
Chocolate cream
Bread and butter.

January 4th :

Fresh fruit
White beans
Spinach with hard boiled eggs
Steak
Potato dumplings with butter gravy
Lettuce
Bread pudding
Bread and butter

January 5th :

Cooked peaches
Corn
Green peas
Mutton chops
Irish and sweet potatoes
Tomatoes, baked
Lemon pudding
Bread and butter

January 6th :

Fresh fruit
Asparagus
Lettuce
Beef roast
Potato salad
Celery
Apple pudding
Bread and butter

January 7th :

Cooked dried prunes
Vegetable soup
Turnips
Stewed Onions
Smoked ox tongue
Potato pancakes
Mashed Irish potatoes
Lemon cream
Bread and butter

x

APRIL.

April 1st :

Canned fruit
Green corn slices
Spinach with hard boiled eggs
Steak
Fried Irish potatoes
Sliced Tomatoes
Chocolate pudding
Bread and butter

April 2nd :

Fresh fruit
Green peas
Vegetarian ragout
Mutton chops
Artificial chestnuts
Lettuce
Rice pudding
Bread and butter

April 3rd :

Cooked fruit
Carrots
Rice-dish
Veal roast
Mashed Irish potatoes
Baked sweet potatoes
Lettuce
Tutti frutti
Bread and butter

April 4th :

Canned fruit
Vegetable slices
Maccaroni dish
Beef roast
Potato dumplings
Sweet potatoes
Celery salad
Charlotte russe
Bread and butter

April 5th :

Fresh fruit
Pea soup
Cabbage with apples
Corn with okra
Onions
Veal chops
Fried Irish potatoes
Red flammery
Bread and butter

April 6th :

Canned fruit
Spinach with eggs
Artificial chestnuts
Steak
Green corn
Sweet potatoes
Irish potatoes
Prune pudding
Bread and butter

April 7th :

Cooked fruit
Dried peas with fried onions
Asparagus
Corn dumplings
Irish potatoes
Celery salad
Orange cream
Bread and butter

xi

JULY.

July 1st :

Canned fruit
Green beans
Rice with apples
Mutton roast
Mashed Irish potatoes
Bean salad
Lemon jelly
Bread and butter

July 2nd :

Cooked fruit
Cucumbers
Pea slices
Veal chops
Tomato dish
Fried Irish potatoes
Vanilla pudding
Bread and butter

July 3rd :

Fresh fruit
Cabbage
Maccaroni
Steak
Potato pancakes
Sweet potatoes
Lettuce
Chocolate pudding
Bread and butter

July 4th :

Cooked fruit
Bean soup
Egg plant
Mushrooms
Sauerkraut
Mutton Chops
Mashed potatoes
Celery
Flammery
Bread and butter

July 5th :

Fresh fruit
Vegetable ragout
Green beans
Tomatoes
Steak
Fried Irish potatoes
Mixed fruit compote
Bread and butter

July 6th :

Fresh fruit
Rice dish
Pea slices
Cauliflower
Beef roast
Potato dumplings
Almond pudding with fruit juice
Bread and butter

July 7th :

Fruit compote
Noodles
Spinach with eggs
Mushrooms
Veal chops
Irish potatoes
Sliced tomatoes
Puekler ice cream
Bread and butter

OCTOBER.

October 1st :

Fresh fruit
German kale
Sweet corn
Sliced tomatoes
Steak
Mashed potatoes
Apple pudding
Bread and butter

October 2nd :

Canned fruit
Rice soup with tomatoes
Spinach with sliced eggs
Stewed chestnuts
Fried Irish potatoes
Fried chicken
Baked sweet potatoes
Celery
Tutti frutti
Bread and butter

October 3rd :

Fresh fruit
Green peas
Turnip greens
Stewed tomatoes
Smoked ox-tongue
Bread pudding
Bread and butter.

October 4th :

Apple sauce with canned peaches
Kohlrabi
Oyster plant
Sliced Irish potatoes, fried
Lettuce
Steak
Rice pudding
Bread and butter

October 5th :

Fresh fruit
Carrots
Green peas
Rice
Irish and sweet potatoes
Sliced tomatoes
Veal chops
Chocolate pudding
Bead and butter

October 6th :

Canned peaches
Spinach with eggs
Corn
Beet salad
Celery
Stewed chicken
Mashed potatoes
Rice pudding
Bread and butter

October 7th :

Rhubarb compote
Green beans and corn
Cabbage with apples
Fried ham
Irish potatoes
Chocolate cream
Bread and butter

COOKING RECIPES

SOUPS.

REMARKS.

In using the yolks of eggs in soups, care must be taken that they do not harden in lumps in the soup. In order to avoid this, first beat them well and stir into them a few tablespoonfuls of the soup and beat together until thoroughly mixed and smooth ; then pour this into the soup.

1. VEGETABLE SOUP STOCK.

1 onion, 2 potatoes, 1 egg, 1 stick of celery, 2 carrots, 1 slice of egg plant, 1 slice of squash, a handful of black-eyed peas (fresh or dried), a little parsley, a handful of asparagus, and 2 ozs. of butter.

After having washed the vegetables, cut all into pieces and stew in the heated butter for a while; then add a little boiling water and boil till done, after which stir all through a sieve. This vegetable stock is used for a number of soups.

2. VEGETABLE SOUP.

Green peas, snap beans, carrots, cauliflower, celery, onions, parsley, kohlrabi, potatoes, squash, black-eyed peas (in shell).

Put butter in a pot on a fire, when heated stir into it one-half tablespoonful of flour until it is a dark yellow, pour boiling water to it, a little salt, and all or most of the above named vegetables (which have been washed and cut) and boil till done. Finally, just before serving, add the yolks of three eggs.

3. SPLIT PEA SOUP.

Put 4 oz. of split peas in cold water and boil till done, and then put them through a sieve. Meanwhile fry a spoonful of fine cut onions in 1 1-2 oz. of butter and add to it the necessary amount of soup vegetables, the strained peas and a little salt, and boil a while. Serve with dices of toast.

The same soup may be made with black-eyed peas and green peas.

4. PEA SOUP.

1 pint of green peas (or French peas). Boil with 3 oz. of butter over a moderate fire; sprinkle 1 1-2 or 2 tablespoonfuls of flour over it, add the necessary amount of water, a little salt and vegetable stock and boil till done. Add the yolks of 2 eggs and serve over slices of toast.

5. WHITE BEAN SOUP.

1 lb. of white beans, 1 1-2 oz. of butter, 1 3-4 oz. of flour, salt, vegetable stock.

Wash the beans and put them in rain water on a moderate fire; boil till done and then stir through a hair sieve. Brown the flour, add the beans, salt and vegetable stock. If too thick add a little warm water; boil one-half hour longer and just before serving drop in toasted bread cut in squares or dice.

6. WHITE BEAN SOUP WITH PARSLEY.

Wash the beans and put them on the fire in cold rain water. Add celery and onions, let boil till done, then stir through a fine sieve; add salt, browned flour,

the juice of a lemon, fine chopped parsley. Put into
the soup finally square or dice-shaped pieces of toast,
and serve.

7. ASPARAGUS SOUP.

Peel 1 lb. of cut and washed asparagus and boil
in salted water or beef soup till done.   Melt 3 oz. of
butter in a pan, add 2 tablespoonfuls of flour, stir a
while and then add the water of the asparagus; let it
boil a while and then put in the asparagus. Before
serving beat the yolks of two or three eggs in the
tureen. Add eight or ten spoons of the soup, being
careful to beat continually the yolks to prevent hard-
ening. Then add the rest of the soup and strew over
it fine chopped parsley.

8. CAULIFLOWER SOUP.

This soup is made like No. 7.   Except that
before serving, lemon juice, to taste, may be added.

9. GREEN CORN SOUP.

Boil 3 or 4 oz. of green corn in a little water
slowly for four or five hours, now and then adding a
little more water. Stir through a fine sieve, let it
come to a boil again, adding salt, vegetable stock and
1 1-2 oz. butter. If the soup is too thin thicken with a
teaspoonful of flour dissolved in milk and pour it into
the soup, stirring the while. Before serving add the
yolk of 1 egg and farina dumplings.

10. SPINACH SOUP.

Clean and wash one-half peck of spinach; boil in a
little water; put 1 1-2 oz. of butter in a pot, add the
spinach and boil for a while; add a little salt, 2 tablespoonfuls of cornstarch and as much water as is
needed. Serve with little crackers.

A soup may be made in the same way of squash.

11. TOMATO SOUP.

Wash and boil 2 lbs. of tomatoes; when done stir through a hair sieve; beat one-quarter lb. butter mixed with 2 tablespoonfuls of cornstarch and stir into tomato stock, together with a little salt, naehr-salz size of a pea, (see preface). Add the necessary amount of water and some parsley, chopped fine; after boiling 20 minutes longer, take from the fire, and before serving pour into it one-half pint of cider.

12. PEANUT SOUP.

Peel and grate 4 oz. of peanuts ; put 1 quart of buttermilk on a moderate fire ; stir constantly until it comes to a boil, then pour it over the grated peanuts : add a little salt, sugar and 1-2 tablespoonful of meal, and let boil 20 minutes, stirring all the while ; take from the fire, add the yolks of 2 eggs.

13. BREAD SOUP.

Soak 1 lb. of stale white bread, whole wheat or graham bread, over night in cold water and boil it with this water till done : meanwhile wash and scald 1-4 lb. of seedless raisins, add them to the salt, sugar and pint of milk to the bread, which has been well stirred ; boil all for 10 minutes longer and serve the soup with the juice of a lemon or a cup of cider.

14. POTATO SOUP.

Cut into pieces 1 1-2 lb. peeled and washed pota-toes ; boil them in salted water till done and then put with the same water through a sieve. Meanwhile fry a tablespoonful of onions cut fine and 1 tablespoonful of flour to a light brown in 2 oz. of butter; pour cold water to it ; add the vegetable stock to the pota-toes.

15.   LENTIL SOUP.

Soak 1 lb. of lentils over night in rain water ; next morning put them over a moderate fire in the same water in which they were soaked, and cook till thoroughly done.   If needed, add cold rain water now and then ; put through a hair sieve ; brown one tablespoonful of flour and one-half fine chopped onion in 2 oz. of butter and stir into the soup.   Salt to taste.

16.   CARROT SOUP.

Cut into pieces 1 1-2 lbs. of cleaned and washed carrots; boil them in water with a little chopped onion and parsley and 1 1-2 oz. of butter till well done.   Meanwhile stir 1 tablespoonful of flour into 1 1-2 or 2 oz. of melted butter (having put the carrots through a sieve) and boil again for a few minutes. Serve with farina dumplings.

17.   MUSHROOM SOUP.

Wash 1 lb. of mixed mushrooms, chop them, not fine, add 3 oz. of butter, one-half onion, a little fine chopped parsley.   Stew slowly a while, adding the necessary amount of water and boil till done.   Brown a little flour in butter, add it to the soup and stir into it, just before serving, the yolks of 2 eggs.

18.   WHITE CABBAGE SOUP.

Shave 1 lb. of white cabbage fine; cook till well done, add to it a little salt, 1 tablespoonful of cornstarch, dissolved in cold water, 2 tablespoonfuls of fresh butter, 1 egg, one-half bottle of cider and serve with snowflake crackers.

19.   PRUNE SOUP No. 1.

Wash prunes (fresh or dried) in cold water and cook in a little cold water over a moderate fire till done; put them through a sieve and sweeten to taste.

In another pot, put about one quart of milk and mix with it 2 or 3 tablespoonfuls of cornstarch and bring it to a boil, stirring all the while. Salt to taste, let it boil a few minutes longer and take from the fire. Just before serving stir the prunes into the milk.

20. PRUNE SOUP No. 2.

This soup is made like the above, except that the prunes are not put through a sieve, and flour is used instead of cornstarch.

21. CHERRY SOUP.

Wash and pit sour cherries; boil them in a little water and sugar till done. Meanwhile, or the day before, soak stale bread in cold water till soft; put this on a moderate fire with the juice of one lemon and the peel of one-half a lemon and a little salt; let boil ten minutes, stirring constantly; then put the cherries into it and set aside.

22. APPLE SOUP.

2 quarts of apples, one-half pint of white wine, water, sugar and tapioca.

Cut the apples into pieces, unpeeled, wash them and boil them in a little water till well done. Put them through a sieve, pour water on this sauce and let boil again for a few moments. Stir 2 tablespoonfuls of tapioca with the wine and sugar to the soup and boil one or two minutes longer.

23. PEAR SOUP.

Wash and cut the pears in pieces and boil in water till done. Stir through a sieve, put over the fire, mix some cornmeal or flour, then sweeten to taste.

24. BLACKBERRY SOUP.

1 quart of blackberries, 1 1-2 quart of water, lemon juice, sugar, 1 tablespoonful of tapioca.

Wash the blackberries and boil one-half hour in water, after which put them through a sieve. Put them on the fire again, add sugar and lemon juice to taste, and finally the tapioca; boil five minutes longer and just before serving pour into the tureen over dice-shaped pieces of toast.

25. BUTTERMILK SOUP.

Cook 2 cups of pearl barley with one-half table-spoonful of flour till well done. Bring to a boil 1 quart of buttermilk with one-half tablespoonful of flour, stirring constantly; add the barley and salt, sweeten to taste, and add one egg just before serving.

26. BARLEY SOUP.

One-half lb. prunes, 2 cups of barley; boil each alone till well done in a little water; salt and sweeten to taste; add a little butter and 1 quart of milk, bring to a boil and take off.

27. CHOCOLATE SOUP.

Bring to a boil 1 quart of milk, add to it 1 table-spoonful of flour dissolved in milk, 2 cups of grated chocolate, a very little salt and sugar, bring to a boil while stirring. Before serving, the yolk of an egg may be added. Serve with crackers.

28. RICE SOUP.

Put 4 oz. of rice in water and heat till just before the boiling point, then pour the water off and add fresh cold water to it; boil slowly with 1 tablespoon-ful of butter till well done. Meanwhile stir 1 tea-

spoonful of flour in a cup of milk, pour this with some
vegetable stock into the boiling rice; salt to taste and
cook for 15 minutes longer, stirring all the while.
Before serving add the yolks of 2 eggs.

29. OATMEAL SOUP.

1 large cup of oatmeal, ¹⁄₂ cup of butter. 1 quart
of water, salt and vegetable stock.

After having melted the butter, stir the oatmeal
into it; when well mixed add the water, vegetable
stock and salt, boil all well done and serve. If desired
any kind of fruit juice may be added to the soup.

30. QUAKER OATS SOUP.

Bring 1 quart of milk to a boil, then pour into it
slowly 1 quart of Quaker Oats; let it boil 20 minutes,
stirring constantly; salt and sweeten to taste, take off
and serve.

31. FARINA SOUP.

Bring to a boil ¼ lb. of washed seedless raisins,
or ¼ lb. of currants and raisins mixed, in a little
water; season with a litte lemon spice (see preface)
and salt. Add slowly while stirring constantly, 1 cup
of farina. Cook 10 minutes, take off, and just before
serving, add 1 egg well beaten; sweeten to taste and
flavor with juice of a lemon and a cup of cider.

This soup may be made with cornmeal, pearl
barley, green corn or rice instead of farina.

32. BROWN SOUP No. 1

In a deep, dry pan, brown very evenly, stirring
constantly, 1 cup of flour; when of a chocolate brown,
pour cold water on it; season with salt and 2 teaspoonfuls of butter and take off. This is particularly
good for convalescents.

33. BROWN SOUP No. 2.

This is made like the above except that half milk and half water is used; add 2 eggs well beaten and flavor with lemon spice and sugar to taste.

33a. BEEF SOUP.

Take 3 lbs. of lean meat of the leg, or two ox tails, cut in small pieces, and put with cold water and a little salt on a moderate fire, scum and let boil for 4 hours. Then strain through a fine sieve, put the fluid on the fire again, put some fine cut celery and parsley into it ; add either rice or soft boiled barley, beans, lentils or peas; so much of either of these must be added to make the soup pretty thick.

34. CRANBERRY SOUP.

Take 6 cups of cranberry sauce; add to it 1 cup of ginger bread or ginger snaps soaked in water; add salt and sugar to taste and 1 teaspoonful of corn-starch dissolved in a little water, and boil a while: take off and serve with toast or crackers.

This soup may be made with musk mellon, raspberry sauce, or gooseberry sauce, instead of cranberries.

COLD SOUPS.

35. PEACH SOUP No. 1.

Peel and cut into pieces, 2 lbs. of very ripe peaches ; strew sugar over them and pour on a mixture of half cider and half water ; let stand an hour and serve with vanilla wafers.

36. PEACH SOUP No. 2.

This is made like the above except that hard peaches are used ; they are brought to a boil with water and sugar over a quick fire ; then pour into a tureen. When cold add cider to taste.

37. CHERRY SOUP.

Wash and boil 2 lbs. of cherries in water for 20 minutes ; sweeten to taste. When cold serve with crackers.

38. STRAWBERRY SOUP.

Wash 1½ lbs. of strawberries, put them in a bowl, strew well with sugar and pour over them a mixture of water, the juice of a lemon, and 2 cups of cider. Serve 2 hours later with lady fingers.

39. PINEAPPLE SOUP.

Grate a peeled pineapple ; pour over it 1 pint of water and 1 pint of cider ; sweeten to taste and serve with lady fingers.

40. RASPBERRY SOUP.

Take 1 quart of raspberries, wash them if necessary, and stir through a hair sieve ; pour over them a mixture of 1 quart of water and the juice of 2 lemons. Sweeten to taste, put spiceless wafers in the tureen and pour the soup over.

This soup may be made with blackberries instead of raspberries.

41. HUCKLEBERRY SOUP.

Wash 2 lbs. of huckleberries ; put them in water, bring to a boil and stir through a fine hair sieve into a bowl in which is 3 oz. of sugar and ½ bottle of cider. Serve with dice-shaped pieces of toast.

42. CLABBER SOUP.

Put fresh milk in a bowl in a moderately warm place for 1 or 2 days till it turns to clabber; sprinkle over it sugar and grated brown or graham bread, a little cinnamon and grated ginger snaps.

43. ALMOND MILK SOUP.

Take 4 oz. of sweet almonds, and 8 oz. of bitter almonds, blanch and chop them fine, then boil them in 3 quarts of sweet milk in which is 1 peach leaf or lemon spice to taste, for ½ hour; add a tablespoonful of cornstarch mixed in a little of the cold sweet milk, a little sugar and salt and boil a while. Stir into the soup the well beaten yolks of 2 eggs; when cold take out the peach leaf; beat to a stiff froth the whites of the 2 eggs and from a spoon drop lumps of the froth at regular distances over the top of the soup. Serve cold with crackers or toast.

44. VANILLA SOUP.

This is made like the above except that vanilla is used for flavoring instead of a peach leaf, and the almonds are omitted and a little more cornstarch is used.

45. PECAN SOUP.

This may be made the same as the almond soup except that pecans are used instead of almonds.

46. CURD SOUP.

Stir 1 lb. of curd through a hair sieve and add 2½ oz. of sugar; pour into the curd 1 quart of cream, being careful to beat the curd hard and constantly while pouring in the cream that it may be light and foamy. Serve with grated ginger bread.

47. RICE SOUP.

Blanch and chop fine 1½ oz. of pecans; boil them

in 1 quart of milk for 10 minutes and add 1 cup of rice flour or rice meal ; let it boil slowly for a while, take off and sweeten to taste. Before serving beat into it the yolks of 2 eggs.

48. SAGO OR TAPIOCA SOUP.

This soup is made the same as the above except that instead of rice, sago or tapioca may be used, omitting the pecans.

49. CIDER SOUP No. 1.

Take 1 bottle of cider and the same amount of water ; add to this 1 cup of seedless raisins soaked in hot water, sugar to taste, the juice of 1 lemon, rind of ½ lemon, 2½ lbs. of grated stale graham bread or whole wheat bread ; let it stand for 2 hours, stirring now and then.

50. CIDER SOUP No. 2.

Mix 2 tablespoonfuls of cornstarch with a little water to dissolve it, stir it into a pint of boiling water ; add sugar to taste, a little salt and lemon spice ; boil 10 minutes, stirring constantly; take off and when cold add the juice of a lemon and 1 bottle of cider. Serve cold with macaroons.

BREADS.

51. SOFT OATMEAL BREAD.

Take 1 pint of oatmeal that is left from breakfast ; stir into it ½ pint of scalded milk ; when well mixed add ½ cup of yellow cormeal ; when partly cold add quickly the yolks of 3 eggs, and then stir in the well beaten whites ; cover the bottom of the baking pan with chopped dates, pour over the bread mixture and bake in a quick oven 30 minutes. It should be broken with a fork and taken out with a spoon.

52. MUSH GEMS.

Stir ¾ of a cup of cornmeal with a pint of hot milk and boil till smooth ; take from the fire, add the yolks of 4 eggs and then the well beaten whites. Bake in greased gem pans in a moderate oven 20 minutes.

53. BREAD STICKS.

Sift into a large bowl a quart of whole wheat flour ; rub into it 2 teaspoonfuls of good butter until it is thoroughly mixed with the flour ; now stir briskly with a large spoon while pouring in with the other hand ½ pint of cold water ; this must now be kneaded into a firm, smooth dough ; cut off a piece the size of a small fist and roll it on the bread board until it is about the thickness of the little finger and cut into 5-inch lengths ; put all in a long baking pan, being careful that they do not touch each other, and bake 1 hour, turning occasionally with a fork. The colder the dough is while working the closer and more tender the bread sticks will be.

54. MUFFINS OF WHITE FLOUR.

Mix together 2 tablespoonfuls of milk, 2 tablespoonfuls of butter, 2 teaspoonfuls of sugar, yolks of 2 eggs, 1 teaspoonful of salt, 2 teaspoonfuls of baking powder, and stir into it white flour enough to make a dough of proper consistency ; then beat the whites of the eggs, mix all together and put in a well greased pan and bake in a hot oven.

55. CORNMEAL MUFFINS.

These are made the same as white flour muffins,

except that more cornmeal and less white flour is used ; about ?; cornmeal and ¹; white flour.

56. CORNBREAD.

Make this the same as cornmeal muffins, but instead of baking in muffin pans bake in a long pan and when done cut in squares.

56a. RYE BREAD.

Dissolve in the evening 1 compressed yeast-cake in a quart of warm water, mix this with 4 teaspoonfuls of salt and as much rye flour as to make a stiff mass, stir it well and place during the night in a warm place. In the morning knead it well for 1½ hours with wheat flour, form the dough into loaves, put in a warm place to rise and bake them for 1½ hours in a good hot oven. It ought to have a good broad crust.

56b. WHOLE WHEAT BREAD.

This is made like the above, except a little less wheat flour is used.

VEGETABLES.

57. VEGETABLE RAGOUT.

This mixture is made of equal parts of boiled Irish potatoes cut in small square pieces, raw apples, cooked beets (cut fine), and a few seedless raisins.

Make a gravy of 1 tablespoonful of white flour, 1 tablespoonful of butter and let come to a boil ; add salt and water, and put the vegetables, with Dr. Lahmann's naehrsalz (see preface), and juice of ½ lemon into it and let all come to a boil again before serving.

58. CABBAGE WITH APPLES.

Chop ½ of a large cabbage very fine, boil it in a very little water with a little salt, good drippings and ¼ tablespoonful of butter. When half done add 3 large or 5 small cooking apples (peeled and sliced) to the cabbage till they are done. Pour over it the juice of ½ lemon and a little flour mixed together and let boil a while longer.

Red cabbage may also be used for a change in the same way.

59. CABBAGE WITH POTATOES.

Clean the cabbage leaves and cut in large pieces like lettuce and put with the necessary amount of boiling water on the fire till done ; then peel and cut in pieces some Irish potatoes and add them to the cabbage and let boil till done. Season with good drippings, butter and salt ; strew over a little flour, mix all well together adding water when necessary ; put in some beef drippings and let it boil for a few minutes longer.

60. SAUERKRAUT.

Put 2¾ oz. of butter or nutcoa in a pot with a little boiling water ; add 1 lb. of sauerkraut and boil till done ; then add 2¾ oz. of beef drippings, a few small, cooked Irish potatoes, a little flour and Lahmann's naersalz (as much as 3 peas); put this with the cabbage with the necessary amount of water and mix well together a while.

61. SPINACH.

Take a peck of spinach and wash clean ; put it in a very little boiling water, adding water when necessary ; when well done take up and if so preferred, chop fine ; this is a matter of taste. Make a gravy of

10 oz. of butter with ½ chopped onion and bread crumbs ; put the spinach into it and add sweet milk to taste.

Beet leaves may be used in the same way.

62. ONIONS.

Peel the onions and put them on the fire with butter, salt, a little nutmeg and grated zwieback ; add a little water when necessary, flavor with lemon juice to taste and serve when done.

63. CARROTS.

After having cleaned and washed 2 bunches of carrots, cut them in small thin strips about 2 inches long and put them with a tablespoonful of butter or nutcoa, with a little water on a moderate fire and when done sprinkle over the carrots a little flour, salt and sugar to taste, and chopped parsley ; let all boil together in the necessary amount of water, slowly, for a few minutes.

64. GREEN BEANS.

Take 2 quarts of green beans and break in two or three pieces ; after having washed the beans put them with ½ tablespoonful of beef drippings with a cupfull of boiling water and boil till done. Meanwhile make a gravy of ½ tablespoonful of butter, 1 tablespoonful of flour, ½ chopped onion and the necessary amount of water and salt to taste ; put the beans into it and let all come to a boil again.

65. WHITE BEANS.

After having shelled 2 quarts of beans, boil in a little water for several hours till done ; then make a gravy with a little butter, ¼ tablespoonful of flour, salt and water and add to the beans ; pour over the beans a little milk so they will not be too dry.

66. CUT BEANS.

String very young, green beans and cut them in thin length-wise pieces, wash these and mix with them butter, salt, ½ onion chopped fine, and a very little water. Boil until done ; add water to them when necessary, mix a little flour in with the beans and boil together.

67. BEETS.

Boil the beets till done, but do not stick them with a fork or they will lose their fine red color ; then cut in round slices and stew them with butter and a little lemon juice.

68. KOHLRABI.

Peel and cut 1 peck of kohlrabi in round fine slices and boil in little water till done ; take off and cool and if there is too much water pour off in another pan ; then make a gravy with this water, 1 pint of milk, salt, Lahmann's naehrsalz, ½ tablespoonful of flour and a tablespoonful of butter ; add this gravy to the kohlrabi and let all come to a boil again. If the kohlrabi is young and has greens, cut and boil both together.

69. LETTUCE.

Clean, wash and cut 4 to 6 large heads of lettuce, do not cut them too fine ; put them in boiling water and boil till done ; then make a gravy of 2 oz. of butter, 1 pint of water, 1 pint of milk, a small, chopped onion and ½ tablespoonful of flour ; put the lettuce in this gravy and let all come to a boil together.

70. WHITE TURNIPS.

Take ½ peck of nice, sweet, white turnips, peel and cut them in pieces ; make a gravy of 1 tablespoonful of good beef drippings or butter, milk and salt and put the turnips into it ; bring all to a boil till well done, and add as often as necessary, a little milk or cream and mix well together before serving.

71. WAX BEANS.

These beans are to be cooked just like the green beans except that milk instead of water is used and the onions are omitted.

72. GREEN PEAS AND CARROTS.

After having shelled the peas put them in boiling water and boil till done ; then cut the carrots into small length-wise pieces and boil seperately till done ; then mix the peas and carrots together and make a sauce by pouring over them a very little flour, a little salt, sugar to taste and parsley chopped fine ; mix all well together and serve.

73. CAULIFLOWER.

Cut off the stalks and take out the little leaves with a small knife so that the head of the cauliflower does not break in pieces ; put them in cold water a while to clean, and then put it on the fire with a little salt in the water to boil till done ; pour off the water, which is to be used for the sauce, and serve with cream, sauce or melted butter.

73a. TURNIP GREENS WITH POTATOES.

Strip the leaves of a bucket-full of turnip greens from the stems ; wash these well and cut them fine ; put with ½ pint of water on the fire together with a piece of bacon and some salt ; boil till nearly done, then add a large, grated raw potato and ½ cup of milk and let boil 15 or 20 minutes longer, Must not be watery but fluid evaporated.

73b. GERMAN KALE.

Wash and cut the kale and boil in ½ pint of

water till half done. Meanwhile cook in another pot a piece of beef, ham or bacon ; when done mix it with the kale and sprinkle a little flour over it ; mix well, let fluid evaporate and serve.

74. CAULIFLOWER WITH CHEESE.

After having cooked the cauliflower as in the above plain cauliflower, serve nicely in a deep dish ; mix the cream sauce with 1 or 2 tablespoonfuls of grated parmesan or Swiss cheese; pour it over the cauliflower and cover entirely with cheese and melted butter and brown in a hot oven.

75. OYSTER PLANT.

Take a tablespoonful of flour and mix well with water or milk ; clean each piece of the oyster plant in hot water and peel ; cut in 2 or 3 inch lengths and boil in the above gravy till done ; add the necessary amount of butter, salt and sugar, and before serving sprinkle over bread crumbs.

76. ASPARAGUS.

Peel the asparagus from head to end and cut off as much as is hard ; wash them and tie in small bundles ; put in boiling water, enough to cover, and boil very slowly, otherwise the softer parts will cook to pieces before the rest. Season with a very little salt so as not to harden the asparagus. Serve with melted butter or asparagus gravy.

77. CUCUMBERS.

Take 4 long, slender cucmbers, peel them, take out the seeds and cut in length-wise pieces and stew in water seasoned with salt, ½ tablespoonful of butter, and ½ lemon ; instead of lemon use a cup of milk and grated bread crumbs if preferred. Boil ¼ hour.

78. MUSHROOMS.

Cut off a little piece from the ends, wash them carefully and put them on the fire with butter and a little water; let boil slowly ¼ hour, then add a teaspoonful of white flour or grated zwieback, a little salt and lemon juice to the gravy and thicken with the yolk of an egg.

79. CHESTNUTS.

Peel the chestnuts, pour hot water over them and take off the inner skin ; season with a little salt, sugar and butter, and boil till done ; then add a little flour and mix together.

80. DRIED WHITE BEANS.

Soak them over night in cold water, then put on the fire and boil ; change the water twice, then add good beef drippings, a little salt, and when well done, before serving, add lemon juice to taste.

81. DRIED PEAS.

Soak and cook the peas the same as white dried beans ; when done stir through a sieve, season with salt and good beef drippings ; before serving pour over them a gravy of chopped onions browned in butter ; the peas are to be thickened and are good eaten with sauerkraut.

82. DRIED GREEN BEANS IN THE SHELL.

Dry small green beans in the shell during the fall for winter use ; before using soak over night in cold water and then boil in fresh water till done ; add water when necessary, season with salt and lemon juice to taste, and let all boil together for a while.

83. LENTILS.

Put the lentils in cold water to boil till done ; then brown a little cut onion and flour in drippings and butter and mix with hot water, stir this into the lentils and add salt to taste.

84. EGG PLANT.

Wash the egg plant, cut in very thin slices and let them stand in cold salt water ¾ of an hour ; take out and turn each slice in beaten egg and grated bread crumbs and fry in nutcoa.

85. SQUASH.

Peel white or yellow squash, cut in small pieces and boil with very little water till done ; add butter, little nutmeg and lemon juice to taste.

POTATO DISHES.

86. POTATOES WITH MILK SAUCE.

Take medium-sized potatoes ; peel and boil till done ; add the salt just before done, in order not to harden them, so they will not fall to pieces ; pour off the water, make a milk sauce and pour over before serving : make plentifully of the sauce, as good, mealy potatoes are very absorbent.

87. SOUR POTATOES.

Make good beef drippings very hot, brown in it some fine chopped onions and thicken with a little flour ; add the potatoes with water and salt and boil till done. Season with lemon juice to taste.

88. FRIED POTATOES.

Peel and wash small round Irish potatoes ; drain them well and fry on both sides in hot nutcoa, in an open pan ; then sprinkle salt over them, cover the pan and cook till done, shaking the pan often.

Another way to fry potatoes is to boil them with the peel ; take off the peel while they are hot ; put at once in hot nutcoa in an open pan and cook till done on both sides.

The first way is the best, as the potatoes are softer and the flavor finer. If salt is sprinkled over the potatoes while frying they will glisten.

89. MASHED POTATOES.

Boil the potatoes in salted water and put through a sieve ; add butter and milk, or milk and boiling water till the potatoes are of the right consistency ; if agreeable, onions chopped fine or zwieback browned in hot butter may be stirred into the mashed potatoes.

90. STEWED POTATOES.

Boil the potatoes with the peel on, till done, then peel and cut in thick round slices and cover. Meanwhile put about a tablespoonful of butter with a little salt and onion chopped fine, in a hot pan ; add the potatoes to it and stew well ; then stir together the yolk of an egg with lemon juice and parsley chopped fine, and mix all together in the potatoes and let come to a boil.

91. POTATO BALLS.

Boil the potatoes without the peel, till done in salted water ; pour off the water and mash very fine ; add some eggs, butter, a little milk and nutmeg to taste, and form into little round balls ; roll them in grated zwieback and fry in hot butter or nutcoa.

92. POTATO SLICES FRIED.

Peel the potatoes, wash and cut in thin round or length-wise slices, then put half butter and half beef drippings in a pan and put the potatoes in it ; sprinkle with salt, pour over a cup of water and cover ; then let them cook till done and fry a yellow brown.

93. POTATOES FRIED.

Peel, wash and cut the potatoes in pieces 2 or 3 inches long, and dry them well. Meanwhile have heated a deep pan of nutcoa ; put into it the sliced potatoes, and let them cook till a light yellow ; take out with a perforated skimmer ; season with a little salt and serve hot.

94. POTATOES WITH APPLES.

Cook some Irish potatoes alone, also alone the same amount of sour apples ; then mix both together well, mashing as in mashed potatoes ; add salt, good beef drippings, butter and a little sugar to taste, and let come to a boil. Before serving pour over them a thick sauce made of grated zwieback in melted butter.

95. POTATO NOODLES.

Cook irish potatoes till done, then put through a potato masher in wnich they come out like vermicelli; put them in a china baking dish and bake in the oven till done and the top is a light brown.

96. SOUR POTATOES.

Take 1 tablespoonful of nutcoa or butter, 1 table-spoonful of flour, juice of ½ lemon, 2 soft cucumbers, 1 onion, a little salt, Lahmann's naehrsalz, water, and a plateful of sliced raw potatoes.

Brown the flour and the onion, chopped fine, in the melted butter, then add all the other ingredients and boil together till done.

SALADS.

In making a salad it is always best to pour the olive oil over the salad and then mix in the other ingredients.

97. LETTUCE.

Clean, cut and wash the lettuce well in cold water. Just before serving mix with juice of ½ lemon, a little salt and ½ onion chopped fiine.

97a. WATER CRESS.

Prepare just like the lettuce and add hard-boiled eggs chopped fine.

98. BEAN SALAD.

Clean fine green beans, boil till done, then pour off the water and when cool mix with salt, lemon juice, olive oil and fine chopped onion.

99. MIXED SALAD.

Take equal portions of cold, sliced Irish potatoes and beets, and add sliced apples or red cabbage chopped fine, and salted cucumbers ; mix all together (being very careful not to break the slices) with oil, salt, lemon juice and the juice of the beets.

100. POTATO SALAD.

Cook Irish potatoes with the peel, using a kind that are not too mealy ; cut them in thin slices, mix with a little hot water, salt, lemon juice, fine chopped onion or sour cream.

Salads may be made in the same way of beans and cucumbers.

101. SALAD OF WHITE OR RED CABBAGE.

Chop the cabbage very fine, mix with sour cream sauce and serve with potatoes.

102. VEGETABLE SALAD.

Take 1 part of cauliflower, 1 part of carrots, 1 part of peas and 1 part of asparagus tips, and boil each ingredient separately till done ; then mix lightly, put on a large flat plate, cover with mayonaise sauce and serve.

103. CUCUMBER SALAD.

Wash, peel and slice the cucumbers very thin ; just before serving pour over them olive oil, salt and lemon juice, or if preferred, take 1 hard-boiled egg, mash it up very fine with a fork and then stir into it olive oil, salt, lemon juice or sour cream and mix in with the cucumbers.

104. CUBUMBER AND POTATO SALAD.

Fix the cucumbers like the above ; cut boiled Irish potatoes in thin slices ; mix with the cucumbers and finish like the above.

105. CELERY SALAD.

Wash and clean the celery and cut it into 1 or 2 inch lengths, then mix it with mayonaise sauce.

DUMPLINGS.

The white bread which is for dumplings need not be fresh nor put in warm or hot water ; use stale, soak it in cold water and press out the surplus water.

106. FINE POTATO DUMPLINGS No. 1.

Take 2 soup plates full of grated potatoes which have been cooked the day before in the peel ; add 3 tablespoonfuls of flour, a little nutmeg, salt, a small cup of butter, Lahmann's naehrsalz and 4 or 5 eggs; the whites and yolks must be well-beaten separately the whites to a froth; mix all together well; dip out with a tablespoon and drop into boiling, salted water and boil 15 minutes. Serve with melted butter.

107. POTATO DUMPLINGS, No. 2.

To 4 soup plates of grated cooked potatoes, add ½ plate of grated white bread and the crusts cut in pieces and fried in nutcoa, 3 tablespoonfuls of flour, 3 eggs, the whites beaten to a froth, 1½ tablespoonfuls of butter and Lahmann's naehrsalz. Mix all together well; form into round dumplings and cook like the above. Serve with onion gravy.

108. POTATO DUMPLINGS, No. 3.

Take ½ lb. grated potatoes, cooked in the peel, ½ lb. grated white bread, ¼ lb. melted butter, 3 eggs, salt, Lahmann's naehrsalz, and nutmeg; mix this well together with the hands, form into round dumplings and drop into boiling water; boil 15 minutes. Serve with butter or cooked fruit.

109. FINE DUMPLINGS.

1 pint of white flour, 1 pint of grated white bread, 1 pint of beaten eggs and one pint of milk.

Roast the crusts of the bread in a little melted butter; add all the ingredients with 2 tablespoonfuls of butter and Lahmann's naehrsalz; heat it, stirring all the while, till it leaves the pan; when cool enough form into round dumplings, sprinkle with flour and boil 10 minutes well covered. Serve with browned butter and cooked fruits.

110. APPLE DUMPLINGS.

1 soup-plateful of peeled apples cut up, 1 pint of milk, ½ lb. grated white bread, 1 tablespoonful of butter, 4 eggs, whites and yolks beaten separately; sugar and lemon peel to taste.

Mix well together; boil the dumplings in water and salt; pour sugar over them and serve with fruit or vanilla sauce.

111. CORN MEAL DUMPLINGS.

Put 1 pint of milk, ½ lb. of corn meal, salt, and a tablespoonful of butter in a pot on the fire and cook till stiff; pour in a pan to cool a while ; then add nutmeg or grated lemon peel to taste, 3 or 4 eggs, Lahmann's naehrsalz and form into little dumplings like an egg ; cover with grated zwieback and fry in hot nutcoa.

112. PRUNE DUMPLINGS.

Stone and cook sweet prunes with sugar and lemon peel till done ; when cool add a little salt, a little butter, 2 or 3 eggs and as much grated bread as will make them hold together in boiling water ; boil 8 or 10 minutes ; try 1 dumpling first. Serve with firuit or vanilla sauce.

113. CHERRY DUMPLINGS.

These may be made the same as the prune dumplings, except that cherries are used instead of prunes.

114. BUTTER DUMPLINGS.

Take the yolks of 2 eggs, ½ teacupful of milk, 1 cup of flour, ¼ tablespoonful of butter, which is beaten to a froth ; stir all together thoroughly over the fire till it is stiff; take off, let cool, add the well-

beaten whites of the eggs, a little nutmeg and boil
10 minutes ; drop the dumplings into the boiling,
salted water with a tablespoon ; these dumplings are
to be served in different soups, also on the same dish
with green peas.

115. WHITE BREAD DUMPLINGS.

Cream ⅛ lb. of butter ; add and mix well the
yolks of 4 eggs, nutmeg, and if desired, parsley
chopped fine ; soak ½ lb. of white bread in water and
press out the surplus water ; beat the whites of the
eggs stiff and mix all well together ; drop the mixture
from a tablespoon into boiling, salted water, cooking
slowly till done.

116. BREAD BALLS.

Soak a soup-plateful of white bread in milk till
soft, press out the surplus milk ; add sugar, salt and
cinnamon to taste ; form round balls ; turn them in
grated bread crumbs and fry in hot nutcoa.

117. RICE DUMPLINGS.

Wash ½ lb. of best rice, put it in cold water and
boil slowly till well done ; let cool, add 4 eggs, salt,
Lahmann's naehrsalz, 2 oz. of butter well-beaten with
1 tablespoonful of flour ; form into small dumplings
and cook them in boiling water. Serve with tomato
sauce.

118. CLABBER DUMPLINGS.

Mix 1 pint of clabber with 1 pint of grated potatoes cooked the day before ; add 2 eggs, 4 oz. of flour,
salt and caraway seeds to taste ; when well mixed,
boil all together in salted boiling water.

PAN CAKES.

———

Pan cakes are to be fried in equal parts of nutcoa and butter, which makes them more easily digested and they are not so apt to burn in frying.

119. POTATO PAN CAKES, No. 1.

Peel, wash and grate raw Irish potatoes ; add salt, 2 or 3 eggs, onion chopped fine, Lahmann's naehrsalz; mix all together well and bake in little, round, thin cakes in hot nutcoa and butter.

120. POTATO CAKES, No. 2.

Grate fresh cooked Irish potatoes, mix with them salt, Lahmann's naehrsalz, and bake like No. 115. Potatoes that have been cooked for dinner may be used but they will not be so nice.   In case you use the cold potatoes add 1 or 2 eggs, salt and vegetable iron.

121. EGG PAN CAKES.

For 3 large cakes which fill the pan, take the yolks of 6 fresh eggs, 6 small spoons of flour, 1 pint of sweet milk, 2 pints of sour cream and a little salt.

Beat the yolks, cream, flour and salt together well, then stir in the milk.   Just before baking add the well-beaten whites of the eggs.

122. CORNSTARCH PAN CAKES.

Take yolks of 4 eggs, 2 oz. of cornstarch, 1 pint of warm milk, ½ pint of water and a little salt; beat all together well; add the well-beaten whites and bake in hot butter and nutcoa.

123. FLOUR PAN CAKES.

For a medium sized pan cake which covers the

pan, take ⅛ lb. of flour, 2 eggs, 1 pint of milk and little salt ; beat all well together and bake in hot butter and nutcoa.

124. CURRANT PAN CAKES.

3 eggs, 2½ tablespoonfuls of flour, 1 pint of sweet milk mixed with a little water, a little salt and sugar. Beat well. Put nutcoa and butter in a pan ; when hot put in the batter ; pour over it the washed currants with sugar to taste. Before turning pour over the currants fine grated zwieback and serve on this side sprinkled with sugar.

125. SOUR CHERRY PAN CAKES.

May be made the same as above except that cherries are used instead of currants.

126. APPLE PAN CAKES, No. 1.

Peel and cut in thin slices a soup plate full of nice ripe apples. Put in a pan and cover with a little butter. Pour over them the batter (as in currant pan cake); let bake till done. Turn and bake without zwieback. Serve with sugar sprinkled over it.

127. APPLE PAN CAKE, No. 2.

Make a batter as in No. 124 ; put in a pan with hot butter ; strew over this the peeled, sliced, ripe, sour apples, with sugar to taste. Cover for a while till done ; take off after having turned and baked the other side.

128. LITTLE APPLE PAN CAKE, No. 3.

Peel and cut in thick, round slices, ripe, sour arples ; turn each slice in well-beaten batter made of eggs, milk, flour, salt and a little sugar and bake in hot butter or nutcoa.

129. APPLE PAN CAKES, No. 4.

Take 2 tablespoonfuls of flour, ½ cup of sweet milk, yolk of 3 eggs, a little salt and a little sugar. Beat all together well. Meanwhile cook some sour apples and stir them through a sieve. Add sugar and lemon juice and pour over the cake (which has been baked of half the batter). Then bake another cake and put the unbaked side next to the pan cake with apples and serve with sugar.

130. PRUNE PAN CAKES.

Take a batter as in No. 124, put it in a pan with hot butter and nutcoa for a few moments ; put into this prunes, stoned and cut in half lengthwise pieces, sprinkle sugar over it to taste ; cover for a little while and bake over a moderate fire till done ; then cover the prune side with grated zwieback and bake on this side for a little while. Stew sugar over and serve.

131. PAN CAKES WITH SWEET CORN.

Make a batter as in No. 124 and mix in it fresh, sweet corn left from dinner. Bake in little cakes on both sides in nutcoa. Serve with maple syrup.

132. BUCKWHEAT PAN CAKES, No. 1.

Mix and beat well 2 cups of fine buckwheat flour, 3 cups of hot water, 1 cup of sour cream and salt to taste. Instead of cream 1 cup of grated cold potatoes may be used; then bake immediately in little cakes, and serve with fruit jelly.

133. BUCKWHEAT PAN CAKES, No. 2.

To every cup of buckwheat flour take 1 cup of hot water, 1 cupful of sour cream or little nutcoa or butter, a little salt and ¼ oz. yeast. Dried currants may also be added. After having beaten all thoroughly, set the batter aside to rise. When light, bake like other pan cakes.

134. PAN CAKES WITH JELLY.

Bake little cakes 3 or 4 at once in a pan, like the pan cakes of flour, on both sides, till of a light yellow-brown. Then put on a plate ; spread on each one a tablespoonful of jelly. Double over or roll up and serve.

VEGETABLE SLICES.

135. GREEN CORN SLICES.

Take 1½ cups of green corn, put with it 1 table-spoonful of butter, a little salt and a little cold water and boil it five or six hours till soft. Use as little water as possible, being careful however that it does not burn.

When done take off and let cool. Meanwhile chop an onion fine and fry it in melted butter, add this with 2 eggs a little bread crumbs, salt and Lahmann's naehrsalz to the green corn.

Cut in slices, turn in bread crumbs and fry on both sides in hot nutcoa. Serve with onion gravy.

136. MUSH SLICES.

Use mush, grits, oatmeal or flakes for this nice supper dish. 1½ cup of the cereal, boil till done. Mix them with 1 or 2 eggs, salt, Lahmann's naehrsalz and a little nutmeg. Cut in slices and bake like No. 131.

137. RICE SLICES.

1½ cup of rice boiled in a little water till done. Do not pour off the water ; let it cool and then add 2 or 3 eggs, 1 fine chopped onion fried in butter, chopped parsley, salt, and Lahmann's naehrsalz. Cut in slices and fry like No. 131.

138. SLICES OF VEGETABLES.

Take cold, cooked vegetables, such as spinach, carrots, peas or beans ; chop them, add salt, 3 or 4 eggs, chopped onion, and grated bread crumbs. Fix them the same as the other slices and fry in nutcoa.

139. PEA SLICES.

2 cups of dried green peas soaked over night in cold water. Boil till done, stir through a sieve, add little pieces of white bread, chopped onion heated in melted butter, and 2 or 3 eggs. Cover with grated bread crumbs and fry in nutcoa and butter.

140. TOMATO SLICES.

One dinner-plateful of cooked and grated potatoes, the same amount of peeled, sliced tomatoes, 3 oz. of butter, 2 eggs, salt and Lahmann's naehrsalz. Mix well together ; then bake like the other slices.

VARIOUS

DINNER AND SUPPER DISHES.

141. MACARONI, No. 1.

½ lb. of macaroni cooked with 1½ pints of milk, and ¼ lb. of butter till done. Take off and when cool, add salt, Lahmann's naehrsalz and the yolks of 3 or 4 eggs ; lastly add the well-beaten whites. Stir all together quickly and bake for an hour in a hot oven.

VARIABLE DISHES.

142. MACARONI, No. 2.

Boil the macaroni with water and salt till done ; take from the fire, drain off the water, put into sieve and pour cold water over it. Arrange the macaroni in a layer on the botton of a china baking dish ; sprinkle over this a layer of grated parmesan cheese, a little salt and lumps of butter ; continue these layers of macaroni and cheese, etc., till the dish is full and then sprinkle on top a layer of bread crumbs and butter and bake ½ or ³₄ of an hour, or till done.

143. TOMATOES, No. 1.

Take 7 or 8 tomatoes, cut them in pieces, take out the seeds, and chop in pieces 1 plateful of cooked and grated Irish potatoes, 2 tablespoonfuls of butter, well beaten, mixed with the yolks of 4 eggs, and ¼ lb. grated white bread, salt, Lahmann's naehrsalz and 1 chopped onion. Mix all together thoroughly, add the well beaten whites and bake 1 hour. Serve with tomato sauce.

144. TOMATOES, No. 2.

Peel and slice tomatoes and put a layer of them in the bottom of a china dish. Sprinkle over this a layer of grated bread crumbs, lumps of butter, a little salt and sugar to taste. Continue the layers of tomatoes, bread crumbs, etc. till the dish is full making the top layer of bread crumbs. Bake till done in a hot oven.

145. SOUR CREAM DISH.

Beat ¼ lb. of butter with 1 quart of sour cream till foamy ; then add the yolks of 6 eggs, a little salt,

½ lb. of grated white bread and lastly, the stiff-beaten whites of the eggs. Bake in a china baking dish in a hot oven for 1 hour.

146. CORN MEAL.

Pour ¼ lb. of white corn meal in 1 quart of boiling water, and let it cook slowly for a while ; take off and when cool, add the yolks of 4 eggs, a little salt, Lahmann's naehrsalz, and lastly the well-beaten whites. Put it in a well-greased pan, cover with butter and grated white bread crumbs and boil in hot water.

147. GREEN CORN.

Boil ¼ lb. of grated green corn with 1 pint of milk, slowly till done. Meanwhile soak 3 large zwiebacks or same amount of stale white bread without the crust, in water. Fry 1 onion chopped fine, in 1 large tablespoonful of butter, till brown. Press out the zwieback or bread from the water and mix it well with the corn. Stir in the yolks of 3 eggs; add Lahmann's naehrsalz, salt to taste, and little nutmeg, and finally the well-beaten whites of the eggs. Mix all together thoroughly and put in a pan well greased and lined with bread crumbs, and boil 1¼ hours.

148. CARROTS.

Clean and grate 5 or 8 carrots of medium size. Soak 3 or 5 zwiebacks, or white bread, in milk. Beat thoroughly 1 tablespoonful of good fresh butter and 4 or 6 yolks of eggs. Mix this well with the carrots, add a little sugar and the well beaten whites of the eggs and boil like the above.

149. MUSHROOMS.

Peel, cut and soak 4 zwiebacks or the same amount of white bread in water. Press the water rom the zwieback or bread and put it in a pan with a tablespoon of butter, chopped onion, parsley, salt, Lahmann's naehrsalz. Set it on the stove and let it brown awhile. Meanwhile chop fine ½ lb. of good mushrooms, stew them till tender in a little butter, take off and add 4 yolks of eggs, finally the well-beaten whites of eggs and cook all together in a good gravy. Put all in a pan well greased and lined with bread crumbs and boil for 1 hour in hot water.

150. TAPIOCA.

Put ¼ lb. tapioca with 1 large tablespoonful of butter in 1 pint of boiling water till thick and well-done. When cool add the well beaten yolks of 4 or 5 eggs, 1 teacup of flour and a little nutmeg to taste. Finally add the well beaten whites and cook like the above.

151. SPINACH.

Take 1 can of spinach or the fresh if preferred. Chop it a little with 1 onion, a little parsley and a little salt. Stew it then with one tablespoonful of butter. Meanwhile soak 4 or 5 zwiebacks in milk. Press it out of the milk, mix it with 2½ oz. of butter which has been beaten to a cream and with all the above ingredients. Finally stir in the well beaten whites of the eggs and put all in a well greased pan lined with bread crumbs. Cook 1 hour in boiling water or bake in a china bake dish in the oven.

152. OATMEAL.

Beat 6 oz. of butter to a cream; add to it the yolks of 4 or 5 eggs and 3 oz. of oatmeal. Then cook 3 table spoonfuls of vegetables, such as peas, cauliflower, or asparagus in a little water till done. Pour off the water and mix it with the whites of the eggs, season with a little salt. Mix all together and bake like the above.

153. A POTATO DISH.

Cook and grate 1 lb. of Irish potatoes, beat 4 oz. of butter to a cream to which add the potatoes, yolks of 6 eggs, a little salt, Lahmann's naehrsalz, and nutmeg to taste. Mix all well together ; add finally the well-beaten whites of the eggs and bake in a china bake-dish in a hot oven for 1 hour.

154. RICE DISH.

Boil ½ lb. best rice in a little water till about half done ; then pour off the water. Put a little butter in pan, add to it 1½ quarts of milk and ½ quart of water and let come to a boil. Put the rice in it and cook till done, neither too stiff nor too soft. Add to taste a little salt and sugar. Serve cold or warm.

155. RICE WITH APPLES.

Boil ½ lb. of best rice with 1 quart milk, till about half done. Put a little butter in a pan, put the rice in it, add boiling water and let it cook slowly. When nearly done add the peeled and sliced apples, and sugar to taste ; let all boil together. When necessary shake, but do not stir, so as not to break the rice. Strew sugar over it and serve.

156. TOAST AND CHEESE.

Grate Edam or Swiss cheese and mix with the same amount of butter to a cream, and spread on nicely toasted white bread. Serve hot or cold.

157. PARSLEY ON TOAST.

Cream 3 oz. of butter, add juice of 1 lemon and 3 tablespoonfuls of parsley chopped fine. Mix well together and spread on cold buttered toast.

158. MUSHROOMS ON TOAST.

Stew 2 tablespoonfuls of best mushrooms with a little water and butter. Then put them through a sieve. Beat 3 oz. of butter to a cream, mix it with the mushrooms, stew again and spread on toast or white bread.

159. EGGS ON TOAST.

Chop hard boiled eggs fine; mix a little lemon juice with them and spread on toast or buttered bread.

160. RICE WITH RAISINS.

Soak the rice, pour off the water and put the rice in milk and butter on the fire, and let it boil for 15 minutes. Add a little sugar, salt and seedless raisins and boil till done.

161. ARTIFICIAL CHESTNUTS.

Peel and grate 8 raw Irish potatoes ; add 2 eggs, 1 tablespoonful of butter, bread crumbs and a little salt and sugar to taste. Form into small round balls the size of very small potatoes, turn in bread crumbs and sugar, and boil till done in a pot of boiling nutcoa.

162. CLABBER CREAM.

Beat clabber with the cream on for 15 minutes. Sweeten to taste with sugar ; flavor with cinnamon and fruit juice, and serve with crackers.

EGGS.

163. SCRAMBLED EGGS.

Take to each person 1 egg, 1 tablespoonful of milk, a little salt and ½ tablespoonful of butter. Beat eggs, milk, butter and salt together and cook in melted butter. As soon as it thickens dip out with a spoon in small slices, put in a dish and serve. Instead of butter some prefer to use water in mixing

164. SCRAMBLED EGGS WITH TOMATOES

To 4 or 5 scrambled eggs mix 1 lb. tomatoes stewed in butter and stir through a sieve. Cook again till thick, with salt to taste and ½ onion cut fine if desired.

165. SOUR EGGS.

Take poached or baked eggs for 4 persons over which you pour the following sauce : 2 eggs, 1 teaspoonful of flour or cornstarch, 1 teacup of water and a little lemon juice and a very little sugar if too strong. Let all come to a boil while stirring and mix with ½ tablespoonful of butter and pour over the hot eggs.

166. EGG JELLY.

1 quart of milk, 3 eggs, 4 yolks, the grated peel of a lemon and a little sugar.

Put into a pan, cover and set in a vessel of boiling water and stir till thick. Take it off, sprinkle sugar over and serve with cranberry sauce.

167. EGGS WITH MUSTARD SAUCE.

Cook eggs till hard, cut in 2 halves lengthwise, put them in dish with open side up and sprinkle a little salt over them. Then serve with mustard sauce.

168. EGG CHEESE.

Beat 5 or 6 eggs with 1 quart of milk with a little salt, in a pan on the fire till all is somewhat thickened, but the pan must not be too hot. Pour the eggs quickly, into a dish, that they do not continue to harden. If there is time, it will taste nicer to put the eggs and milk in an earthenware pot set in boiling water till it is thickened.

169. DROPPED EGGS.

Bring to a boil 1 quart of water and 1 pint of lemon juice and a little salt. The eggs are to be cooked in this one at a time. Drop an egg in, take a large spoon and, with this, carefully keep the white covered over the yolk. When the white hardens take the egg out and pour cold water over it.

170. OMELETTE.

Take 1 tablespoonful of flour and dissolve it in 2 tablespoonfuls of tepid milk and the yolks of 4 eggs, a little salt and sugar, and stir all thoroughly together. Finally add the whites beaten to a snow. Bake in a batter pan slowly, on one side, till the dough looks dry ; put on a platter and sprinkle over the half of it the juice of a lemon and some sugar. Double over and sprinkle sugar over.

171. OMELETTE WITH JELLY.

Bake an omelette like the above omitting the lemon juice. When taken up spread raspberry or apple jelly over it. Double over and serve hot.

172. SNOW OMELETTE.

Beat the yolks of six eggs, ½ cup of milk, ½ cup boiling water, 1 tablespoonful of cornstarch, a little salt or lemon juice.

Mix together thoroughly and cook in a buttered pan till dry. Beat the whites to a stiff froth, spread it over the omelette, cover with a hot lid till the whites are hard. Stew a little sugar over, double over, and serve.

173. OMELETTE WITH ZWIEBACK.

Soak some zwieback in milk and then brown it in a pan on the stove in nutcoa or butter till it is a light yellow Make a batter as for the snow omelette and pour it over the zwieback, making cuts in it that the batter may soak through. Then brown the zwieback again on both sides. Put on a plate, sprinkle with sugar or serve with cranberry or other jelly or fruit.

174. EGGS IN CUPS.

Grease the earthenware egg cups with melted butter, break into each cup 2 eggs, sprinkle a little salt over. Have a pan of boiling water on the stove. Set the egg cups in, letting the water cover the cups as high as the eggs in the cups. Let stay in 8 minutes. Take out, let cool in the cups and turn out, or serve hot in the cups.

MEATS.

175. BEEF ROAST.

Put beef drippings in a pan on the top of the stove; beat the beef, rub salt in on both sides, add it then to the drippings with sliced onions, and a little garlic to taste. Let fry on both sides, keeping closely covered all the time. Then put it in the oven to bake and pour the gravy over it every 10 minutes, keeping covered well meanwhile. A roast of 5 lbs. will need to be covered nearly 3 hours. When done take out and sprinkle flour in the gravy to thicken it, and if necessary add a little hot water and boil for a few minutes.

176. VEAL ROAST.

For this roast take, instead of beef drippings, butter and a little bacon without onion or garlic. Cook in the same way as the beef roast, but only 2 hours. Add finally, the gravy with a little sour cream or milk.

177. MUTTON ROAST.

Rub salt into the roast and cook the same as the beef roast.

178. RABBIT STEW.

Wash and cut the meat in small pieces, put in a china dish and pour over it boiled vinegar or lemon juice and water in which is cut onions, spices and bay leaves. Let the meat stay in this spiced vinegar 1 or 2 days. Then take out, put in a pan on the stove with a little of the vinegar, adding water, fresh cut onions, a little salt and flour and let boil till done. Finally thicken the gravy with browned flour, add white wine and a very little sugar to taste.

179. COLD MEAT JELLY.

Take of pork feet and veal feet an equal number ; cook them till done in a little water, salt, cut onions, spices and lemon juice to taste. Take up when done and empty all into a sieve saving the gravy which is drained from the meat. Cut the meat from the feet in small dice-shaped pieces and put in the gravy to cook again till well done. Then pour very cold water in a china dish and empty it out again not drying as this prevents sticking. Pour the meat and gravy into the wet dish, being sure to have gravy enough to cover the meat. Let stand till it is stiff, then cut in slices and serve plain, or it is very nice with mayonaise sauce.

180. FRIED CHICKEN.

Clean and wash the chicken without cutting it up; rub some salt over it and fry it in butter in an open pan till it is a light brown on both sides. Then add a little water, put in the oven and baste with the gravy every 10 minutes. Keep covered, and when done take out of the gravy and carve just before serving. Thicken the gravy with a little flour, and boil a few minutes.

181. STEWED CHICKEN.

Wash and clean the chicken, cut it in pieces and cook till nearly done in boiling salted water. Put some butter and flour (1 tablespoonful for each chicken) in a pot ; add to this a part of the gravy in which the chicken was cooked, and the chicken, and boil together till done. Then take out the chicken and stir into the gravy the beaten yolk of an egg ; pour the gravy over the chicken and serve with cooked rice.

182. STEWED VEAL.

This is cooked like the stewed chicken, except that before well done, a fine chopped onion and capers to taste, is added.

❧

SAUCES FOR
MEATS AND VEGETABLES.
—

183. TOMATO SAUCE.

Wash and boil tomatoes, without peeling, till done ; stir through a sieve, put again on the stove, add butter, little salt, ½ onion chopped fine, and grated bread crumbs ; mix all together well and add sugar to taste.

184. SOUR EGG SAUCE FOR GREEN BEANS AND POTATOES.

Beat the yolks of 2 eggs with 2 tablespoonfuls of best flour and 1 pint of fresh milk ; add ½ tablespoonful of good butter, little grated nutmeg and lemon juice to give a sour taste. Put on the fire with a little salt ; stir continually till done and sufficiently thickened.

185. CAULIFLOWER SAUCE.

Take fresh butter, melt it and add to it ½ tablespoonful of flour, a little fresh milk, salt and nutmeg ;

beat all together well on the fire till thick; take off
and add the well beaten yolks of 2 eggs.

186. ASPARAGUS SAUCE.

Take yolks of 3 eggs, 1½ tablespoonfuls of flour, 3
tablespoonfuls of sweet cream, 1 pint of asparagus
water, or plain water, little nutmeg, juice of 1½
lemons, little sugar to taste. Beat all together and
stir on the fire till it thickens. Take off and stir in
½ tablespoonful of butter and salt to taste.

187. FINE ONION SAUCE, No. 1.

Peel and cut 3 or 4 onions in small pieces and fry
them in a pan with a little piece of fat and 1 tablespoonful of flour till brown ; then add as much water
as is required for the desired amount, and boil slowly
for a while. Stir through a sieve and bring again to
a boil with a little nutmeg and salt. Take off and
stir into it a fresh piece of butter, the yolk of an egg
and a little Liebig's extract of beef.

This sauce is suitable for boiled meats or potatoes.

188. ONION SAUCE, No. 2.

Put beef drippings, with fine chopped onion, on
the fire and let fry till yellow ; add 1 or 2 tablespoonfuls of flour and when grainy, before boiling, add
water till of a proper consistency. Season with a
little salt and lemon juice to taste. Let all boil
together and add ¼ teaspoonful of Liebig's extract of
beef.

189. REMOULADE SAUCE.

Grate 2 or 3 onions and the hard-boiled yolks of
3 eggs, 2 or 3 teaspoonfuls of mustard, 4 tablespoonfuls of best olive oil, 1 tablespoonful of sugar, a little
salt and lemon juice to taste. Beat all together on
the fire, but do not let come to a boil ; then stir through
a sieve, and add ¼ tablespoonful of capers.

190. MAYONAISE SAUCE, No. 1.

½ tablespoonful of butter, yolks of 3 hard-boiled egss, 2¼ tablespoonfuls of finest olive oil, 1 tablespoonful of sugar, little salt and lemon juice to taste.

Cream the butter and add 1 tablespoonful of olive oil, pouring in by drops while stirring and 1 tablespoonful of lemon juice. Beat the yolks alone well with the lemon juice and salt and then mix with the other ingredients.

191. MAYONAISE SAUCE No. 2.

Beat 2 or 3 yolks of fresh eggs, always in one direction, then add ½ small cup of olive oil, pouring in by drops, and beating the while, always in the same direction, till the sauce is thick. Add salt to taste.

192. HORSERADISH SAUCE.

Beat 1 or 2 fresh eggs with lemon juice, olive oil and sugar and salt to taste, for 15 minutes, then add the finely-grated horseradish. This is a good meat sauce.

193. CREAM SAUCE FOR SALADS.

Beat well some thick, sour cream with lemon juice, fine olive oil, a little salt and, to taste, a little fine-chopped onion.

194. CAPER SAUCE.

Put ¼ lb. of butter, 3 tablespoonfuls of flour with water on the fire, and let boil a while, but do not brown ; then add the capers, a little lemon juice and salt.

195. PARSLEY SAUCE.

Chop the parsley fine and stew it in 3 oz. of butter, 3 tablespoonfuls of flour, for 5 or 6 minutes ; then add as much water as desired.

196. MUSHROOM SAUCE.

Take 4 oz. of butter, 3 tablespoonfuls of flour and dissolve in water ;'let stew for a while, then add the juice of 1 lemon, ½ chopped onion, little nutmeg and a little salt. Meanwhile boil the mushrooms in salted water till done ; chop them fine and mix with the other ingredients, adding lemon juice to taste.

197. CUCUMBER SAUCE.

Chop 1 onion fine, stew it in 4 oz. of butter; add cucumbers, peeled and cut in very small squares; let them stew together a few minutes, then sprinkle 2½ tablespoonfuls of flour over them and add water, a little sour cream, salt, Lahmann's naehrsalz, and the juice of 1 lemon and let all boil well together.

SWEET SAUCES.

198. STRAWBERRY SAUCE.

Stir 1 pint of strawberry marmalade through a sieve; add 1 quart of water and lemon juice to taste. If the sauce is desired thicker, stir into the boiling juice 1 tablespoonful of cornstarch dissolved in water and boil again a few moments.

199. RASPBERRY SAUCE.

Boil fresh raspberries with water, stir through a sieve; mix with water, and flavor with lemon juice to taste,

200. CHERRY SAUCE.

Let 1 quart of sour cherries come to a boil with 1 quart of water and stir through a hair sieve ; put the juice again on the stove add sugar to taste and 1 tablespoonful of cornstarch dissolved in water; let come to a boil together and serve hot or cold.

201. PRUNE SAUCE, No. 1.

Wash fresh prunes, stone them and boil with water ; when done stir through a hair sieve ; put the juice again on the fire, add the necessary sugar and cornstarch and let come to a boil.

202. PRUNE SAUNE No. 2.

Stone ½ lb. dried prunes, wash and boil till done in 1 quart of water ; then stir through sieve ; add to this the pulp juice and peel of 1 lemon, and sugar to taste, and put on the fire to boil. If not thick enough stir in a little dissolved cornstarch.

203. APPLE SAUCE, No. 1.

Peel and cut the apples in pieces. 1 quart of water, 1 soup-plateful of sliced apples ; add a few slices of lemon, ½ tablespoonful of butter and boil till done ; stir through a sieve and add ½ cup of washed and boiled currants, and a little dissolved cornstarch.

Prune and apple sauces are nice to serve with dumplings.

204. APPLE SAUCE, No. 2.

This is made like the above except that dried apples are used and ½ the quantity of apples, and twice that of water. Some blanched almonds may also be added, cut lengthwise in half, or grated.

205. CRANBERRY SAUCE.

Boil nice, ripe cranberries in water till done, and stir through a sieve ; add to this sugar and lemon juice to taste.

206. FRUIT FOAM.

Beat the whites of 4 or 5 eggs stiff and mix with
1 quart of fruit juice ; add sugar and lemon juice to
taste.

207. RED CURRANT SAUCE.

Stir 1 pint of washed and cooked currants
through a sieve. Add to the juice ½ lb. of sugar;
beat together for 15 minutes, and serve with cold rice
and blanc mange.

208. FOAM SAUCE.

Take ½ bottle of white wine, 3 yolks of fresh
eggs and two whole eggs, ½ tablespoonful of best
flour, 2½ oz. of sugar, juice and peel of 1 lemon ; put
all together in a steam pot on the fire and stir until
the fluid is foamy.

209. VANILLA SAUCE.

Bring 1 quart of milk with sugar and vanilla to
a boil, then beat well 6 yolks of eggs with a little milk,
(saved from the quart), stir this into the boiling milk,
beating well on the fire for a while but take off before
it comes again to a boil.

210. FOAM SAUCE OF RASPBERRY OR CURRANT JUICE.

Beat 4 fresh eggs thoroughly; add 2 teaspoonfuls
of white flour, 1 quart of fresh raspberry or currant
juice with sugar to taste. Beat well upon the fire till
it puffs up but does not boil. If jelly is used instead
of berry juice, mix and dissolve with ⅓ bottle of white
wine or same amount of water.

211. CHOCOLATE SAUCE.

Put 3 oz. of chocolate in a very little water on the
fire to dissolve, add 1 pint of cream and 1 pint of
sweet milk, a little vanilla and sugar to taste. Take
off and beat in the yolks of 2 eggs.

COMPOTES.

Be careful always in cooking fruits to stir without breaking them. Boil them always on a moderate fire with a little sugar and a little water.

212. GOOSEBERRY COMPOTE.

Clean the green gooseberries from the stems, etc; wash them and boil them in a little water, adding water when necessary. Add sugar and white wine to taste and boil till done. Then stir in 2 eggs well-beaten and take off.

213. HUCKLEBERRY COMPOTE.

Take 2 quarts of huckleberries, clean and wash them, and boil them with water and sugar. Pour a layer of them in the bottom of a china dish and on this a layer of zwieback and continue this till the dish is full. Serve cold.

214. APPLE COMPOTE, No. 1.

Peel and cut good, ripe sour apples and boil with water, sugar and dried currants. The currants and apple slices must remain whole ; when soft take carefully out of the juice, which is to be boiled again with the juice of a lemon and poured back over the compote. Let cool and serve.

215. APPLE COMPOTE, No. 2.

Let apples boil till done as in the above, stir, take off and spread on a flat dish. Beat the whites of 5 or 6 eggs stiff ; mix sugar and cover over the apple compote. Instead of whites of eggs the compote may be garnished with seedless raisins soaked in hot water and blanched almonds cut in thin lengthwise strips.

216.   RHUBARB COMPOTE.

Peel the rhubarb stalk and cut in 2-inch pieces. Boil
slowly till soft, in a little water, with sugar and lemon
juice to taste.   Use 1 glass of water and 4 oz. of
sugar to every ½ lb. of cut rhubarb.

217.   STRAWBERRY COMPOTE.

Clean and wash 1 quart of ripe strawberries ;
cover with 6 oz. of sugar and let stand for several
hours.   Drain off the juice through a collendar ; add
more sugar to the juice, according to taste, and let it
boil till stiff.   Let it cool and then pour over the
strawberries.

218.   PLUM COMPOTE.

Wash and stone nice, ripe plumbs or prunes, put
in a dish with a very little water and a good deal of
sugar.   Cover close and put in the oven to stew for
½ hour.   Then serve with the juice (cold) in a glass
dish.

219.   RED CURRANT COMPOTE.

Bring some sugar and water to a boil ; add to it
the washed and cleaned currants.   Take off and pour
into a collendar.   Take the juice which is drained off,
add more sugar to it and let it boil till it thickens.
When cool pour over the currants.

220.   MIXED FRUIT COMPOTE.

Take equal quantities of currants, strawberries
and cherries ; bring each kind separately to a boil in
sugar and water.   When done mix together and
serve with crackers.

221.   PEACH COMPOTE.

Make a syrup of sugar and water ; add the peeled
fruit and let it boil slowly till done, being careful to

keep the fruit whole. Take off and serve when cool.

222. PRUNE MARMALADE.

5 oz. dried prunes, 2 oz. dried peaches, 2 oz. dried apples. Bring each kind separately, to a boil till done. Stir through a sieve, and put all together, with sugar and lemon juice, on the fire to boil for a while.

223. PLUM COMPOTE.

Clean and stone fresh plums or prunes and let them boil with sugar till done, in their own juice ; then stir through a sieve, add grated bread crumbs browned in butter, sugar, little lemon juice, and let it boil for a while longer.

224. PEAR COMPOTE.

Peel the pears, cut in halves and take out the cores and then put them in water. Meanwhile put a little sugar and butter in a pan on the stove. Add the pears out of the water and let stew for a while until they begin to brown ; then sprinkle over them some sugar ; cover up again until they are a nice brown.

WARM PUDDINGS.

The success of pudding depends largely upon the thorough creaming of the butter, and the beating of the eggs, whites and yolks seperately, and whites always to be added last and beaten as stiff as possible.

The forms or moulds in which the warm puddings are to be baked or boiled must first be well greased with butter and then thickly sprinkled over with very finely grated bread crumbs. This prevents the pudding from sticking to the mould and forms an agreeable crust.

Before using cornstarch always dissolve it in a little cold water or milk.

225. PLUM PUDDING.

Beat 3 whole eggs and the yolks of 3 eggs, well ; add ½ lb. of flour stirred in 1 quart of milk, 1 lb. of grated stale white bread, ½ lb. of chopped kidney fat, ½ lb. of seedless raisins, ¼ lb. of dried currants and salt to taste ; mix all together thoroughly; put in a form and boil 3 to 5 hours.

226. RICE PUDDING, No. 1.

¼ lb. best rice, 1 pint of milk, grated peel of lemon and juice of ½ lemon, 2 oz. of butter, 2 oz. of sugar, 4 or 5 eggs.

Soak the rice, pour off the water and boil the rice in milk, flavored with lemon peel, till done ; let cool, then add the butter beaten to a cream, the sugar, the yolks of the eggs and the lemon juice, and lastly the whites of the eggs beaten stiff. Lay this mixture and macaroons in layers in a pudding mold, and boil in hot water 2½ hours. This is for 4 to 6 persons.

227. RICE PUDDING, No. 2.

6 oz. best rice, 4 eggs, 2 oz. butter, 2 oz. of sugar, 3 oz. of washed seedless raisins.

Mix and boil this pudding like the above. Instead of raisins, 1½ oz. of finely-grated almonds, which have been beaten in with the butter, may be used. Serve with foam sauce. For 4 to 6 persons.

228. RICE FLOUR PUDDING.

½ lb. of rice flour or corn meal, 1 pint of milk, 2½

oz. butter, 2½ oz. sugar, 6 eggs, the grated peel of ½ lemon or 6 bitter almonds.

Boil half of the milk ; stir into it the remaing half of rice flour or corn meal and half of the butter, and boil, while continually stirring, until it leaves the sides of the pan. Then cream the remaining half of the butter, and, while stirring, add the yolks of the eggs, almonds, sugar and the cooled, cooked flour. Mix in lastly the stiff-beaten whites and boil in a form 2½ hours. Serve with foam sauce. For 5 or 6 persons.

229. SAGO PUDDING.

¼ lb. best sago cooked till thick, in milk, 5 eggs, 2½ oz. of butter, 2½ oz. sugar, 2 oz. grated zwieback, 1 cup of sweet cream and grated peel of 1 lemon.

Mix and cook like the rice pudding No. 1.

230. FOAMY PUDDING.

2½ or 3 oz. of freshest butter, 2½ or 3 oz. of finest flour, 5 eggs, 2 or 2½ oz. of sugar, grated peel of a lemon, ½ pint of milk and 6 macaroons.

Bring the milk and butter to a boil, stir the flour slowly into it, and let boil till it comes from the sides of the pan. When cool add the yolks of the eggs, sugar, lemon peel and finally, while stirring rapidly, add whites of the eggs beaten stiff. Now put half of this mixture in a dish and spread over it a layer of the 6 macaroons, and pour over this the other half of the mixture. Bake 1 hour in a hot oven. Serve with fruit sauce. For 4 to 6 persons.

231. NOODLE PUDDING.

1 quart of milk, 2½ or 3 oz. of butter, 2½ or 3 oz. of sugar, ¼ lb. of noodles, the grated peel of ½ lemon, 1½ oz. grated almonds and a little nutmeg.

Bring the milk, sugar and ½ of the butter to a

boil ; put into it the noodles broken in pieces, let it boil, stirring till the mixture leaves the sides of the pan ; then cream the other half of the butter, add almonds, yolks, the cooled noodles and lastly the stiff-beaten whites of the eggs. Put all in a dish and let boil in hot water or bake in a form in a hot oven. For 4 or 5 persons.

232. VANILLA PUDDING.

¾ lb. stale bread without the crust, 1 pint of fresh cream or milk, 2 oz. of butter, 2½ oz. grated almonds, 2½ oz. sugar, 5 or 6 eggs and vanilla to taste.

Soak the bread in the milk, cream the butter and add the yolks of the eggs, almonds, sugar and vanilla. Beat all the ingredients together for 15 minutes, always in the same direction, and lastly add the stiff-beaten whites of the eggs. Boil 1½ or 2 hours and serve with fruit juice sauce.

233. ZWIEBACK PUDDING.

3 oz. of zwieback, 1 cup seedless raisins, 5 eggs, ¾ quarts of fresh milk, 1½ or 2 oz. sugar and a little nutmeg ro vanilla to taste.

Put some zwieback, several hours before cooking, in the bottom of a pudding mold. Beat the eggs, whites and yolks, together, add them to the other ingredients and pour a layer of the batter over the zwieback and then a layer of zwieback, etc., till all ingredients are put in, in this way, finishing with the zwieback. Boil 1½ or 2 hours and bake in a china dish 1 hour.

234. IRISH POTATO PUDDING.

3 oz. of butter, 3½ or 4 oz. of sugar, ½ oz. finely grated almonds, 6 yolks of eggs, ¾ lb. of cooked grated Irish potatoes, 2 oz. of grated white bread, the grated peel of 1 lemon.

The potatoes shouid be cooked the day before in the peel; cream the butter, add sugar, almonds, lemon peel and then the yolks of the eggs and the potatoes; after beating all together thoroughly, stir in the stiff whites of the eggs and bake at once 1 hour or boil in a mold for 2 hours and serve with a foamy sauce or fruit sauce.

235. SWEET POTATO PUDDING.

Peel and grate 1 large or 2 small raw sweet potatoes; add the yolks of 5 eggs, 1 pint of milk, white wine to taste, a piece of melted butter, sugar, nutmeg and cinnamon to taste. Mix all together well and finally stir in the stiff-beaten whites of the eggs and bake till done about 1 hour

236. BREAD PUDDING WITH ALMONDS.

½ lb. stale, sifted rye bread, or whole wheat bread, ¼ lb. of butter, 8 eggs, ½ lb. sugar, ¼ lb. grated almonds, grated peel of ½ lemon and the juice of 3 or 4 lemons.

Stir the bread in with the butter on the fire ; add the lemon juice, take off and let cool. Then add all the ingredients and finally the stiff-beaten whites of the eggs. Boil the pudding 2 or 2½ hours or bake 1¼ hours. Serve with hot or cold fruit sauce. For 12 or 14 persons.

237. CHOCOLATE PUDDING, No. 1.

2 oz. of butter, 2 oz. of sugar, 6 eggs, 4 oz. grated almounds, 2 oz. of grated chocolate and a little vanilla.

Cream the butter, to which add the sugar, yolks of eggs, almonds, chocolate and vanilla. Stir for 15 minutes ; mix in the well-beaten whites of the eggs and bake for 1 hour in a moderate oven. If to be served cold boil for 2 hours and serve with vanilla sauce. For 5 or 6 persons.

238. CHOCOLATE PUDDING, No. 2.

1 quart milk, ¼ lb. white flour, 4 oz. butter, ¼ lb. unsweetened chocolate, ¼ lb. sugar, ¼ lb. almonds and 6 eggs.

Boil the chocolate with the butter and flour ; take off add the almonds, sugar, yolks of the eggs and finally the stiff-beaten whites of the eggs. Put all in a form which has been greased with butter and sprinkled with grated zwieback and bake for 1 hour. Serve with vanilla souce.

239. CHOCOLATE PUDDING, No. 3.

Cream 2½ oz. butter and mix in with the yolks of 4 or 5 eggs, 1 large teacup of sugar, 2½ oz. of grated chocolate, little vanilla, 6 oz. zwieback soaked in milk and well-drained. Lastly the stiff-beaten whites Bake 45 minutes. For 6 to 8 persons.

240. FRUIT PUDDING.

2 lbs. stale white bread, or zwieback, 1 quart of milk, ¼ lb. butter, 8 or 10 eggs, 6 or 8 oz. sugar, fruit (such as sour apples or cherries lemon peel, lemon juice to taste, ¼ lb. dried currants.

Cut the bread in small pieces, without the crust, mix with the butter and milk and stir in pan on the stove till it comes from the sides of the pan. Let cool, add all the other ingredients and lastly the stiff-beaten whites of the eggs. Put a layer of the batter in a pan to bake, spread a layer of the fruit over this and then a layer of batter, etc., until all the ingredients are used, ending with the batter on top. Cook for 2 hours. For 12 or 14 persons.

241. MACAROON PUDDING.

Cut the macaroons in pieces and put in a pudding mold which has been well-greased ; then strew

in washed, soaked seedless raisins ; pour over all 4 or
5 well-beaten eggs with 3 pints of milk, 2 oz. of
sugar and bake or boil 1 hour.

242. ORANGE PUDDING.

¼ lb. white corn meal, 2 oz. butter, 4 oz. sugar, 3
pints of milk, 5 eggs, 3 oranges.

Let the butter and milk come to a boil ; stir into it
the meal and cook till done. Take off and let cool ;
then add sugar, the yolks of the eggs, the juice and
grated peel of 1 orange ; peel the other two oranges
and lay the sections on the bottom of a well-greased
pan. Cover all with the batter and let bake for ¾ of
an hour.

243 GOOSEBERRY PUDDING.

¼ lb. green gooseberries, ½ lb. sugar, ¼ lb. grated
white bread or zwieback. 6 oz. butter, 6 or 8 eggs, 3
pints of milk.

Boil the gooseberries with half the sugar and a
little water till done ; take off and let stand a day ;
then toast the bread in the butter to a light brown ;
add the milk and boil together till stiff; after it is
cool add the well-beaten yolks of the eggs, the rest
of the sugar and the gooseberries without the juice,
and finally the stiff-beaten whites. Put all in a well-
greased mold or china dish and bake 1 hour. Serve
with the juice of the gooseberries.

244. NUT PUDDING.

30 fresh peanuts or walnuts grated without being
blanched ; then add 6 oz. of bread or zwieback soaked
in milk and drained. Cream the butter with the yolks
of the eggs, the sugar, and ¼ cup of sweet cream.
Mix all together thoroughly adding then the well-
beaten whites and bake in a greased pudding dish

or 1 hour and serve with foam sauce. For 8 or 10 persons.

245. SOUR CREAM PUDDING.

Take 1 quart of sour cream, 6 or 8 eggs, 3 or 4 spoonfuls of flour, sugar, vanilla or lemon peel and juice of 1 lemon and a liittie salt. Beat the cream well ; then add the other ingredients, and finally the stiff-beaten whites and bake for 45 minutes. For 6 or 8 persons.

246. APPLE PUDDING.

Take a tablespplate of sliced sour apples and cover the bottom of a china bake dish whith them. Mix through the apples seedless raisins, or dried currants. Meanwhile melt 2 oz. of butter in a pan and add to it ¼ lb. flour dissolved in 1 cup of milk and let all come to a boil, stirring constantly till it separates from the pan and let cool.

Then cream 2 oz. of butter, add the yolks of 5 eggs, 2 oz. of sugar and the grated peel of 1 lemon. Mix all together with the stiff-beaten whites ; pour all over the apples and bake in an oven for 1 hour. For 8 or 10 persons.

247. PRUNE PUDDING.

1 lb. best prunes, cook till soft ; when cool stone and cut in pieces. Then stir together 1 quart of milk, 3 eggs, 2 oz. of creamed butter, ½ cup of grated zwieback and the juice of the cooked prunes. Mix all together and bake 1 hour.

248. PECAN PUDDING.

Beat 1 tablespoonful of butter to a cream ; add 2 tablespoonfuls of sugar, 3 oz. stale white bread (soaked in water and drained), yolks of 6 eggs and 30 or 40 grated pecan nuts. Finally stir in the stiff-beaten whites of the eggs and bake the pudding for 1 hour in a well-greased form.   Serve with fruit juice.

249.   STRAWBERRY SHORTCAKES.

1 quart of flour, 2 teacupfuls of baking powder, a pinch of salt, 1 tablespoonful of sugar, 3 tablespoonfuls of butter, and milk to make a soft dough. Bake in 2 layers, one on top of the other, with butter between ; when cool split open with a knife and cover with berries sprinkled with sugar ; put the other crust on top and cover with berries.

❦

COLD
PUDDINGS AND CREAMS.

---

250.   RED CORN MEAL PUDDING.

1 quart of raspberry juice, 1 quart of cheery or currant juice, ¼ lb, corn meal and ¼ lb of sugar.

Cook the juice and sugar together, pour the meal into it and let it cook till done but not too stiff.   Then wet a china dish with cold water and pour all into it. When cold turn out into a large plate and serve with vanilla cream and sugar well beaten together.

251.   RED GRITS

Take 1 pint of raspberry juice, 1 pint of water, 3 oz. grits or sago and sugar to taste and finish like the above.

252.   RICE CREAM.

Boil ½ lb. best rice in 1 quart of sweet cream with grated peel of ½ lemon in it.   Beat ¼ lb. of sugar with the juice of 3 lemons, boil till stiff and stir into the ccoked rice, take off from the fire , soak 1 oz. of red gelatine in warm water and add it to the other ingredients. Arrange this with canned or fine cooked fruit in a dish in layers. Let cool till stiff, then turn out on a platter and garnish with fruits.

253. RED FLAMMERY.

5 cups of sweet milk, 3 oz. of sugar, 3 oz. of bitter almonds and 3 oz. of sweet almonds grated, little vanilla or lemon peel and 1 oz. of red gelatine.

Boil the first four ingredients together; add the gelatine which has been soaked in warm water. Rinse a dish out with cold water without drying it and pour all into it to get cold. Serve with fruit juice.

254. HUCKLEBERRY PUDDING.

2 quarts of huckleberries, juice of 2 lemons, juice of 1 quart of huckleberries, sugar to taste, 6 oz. of pearl sago. Cook together the sago juice and berries, and sugar, till the sago is done, stirring all the while. Pour cold water in a dish leaving it wet ; put all in this to get cold ; then turn and serve with crackers.

255. LEMON CREAM, No. 1.

Bring ⅜ of a quart of water with 6 oz. of sugar to a boil, add grated peel of 1 lemon, juice of 3 lemons, yolks of 6 eggs, 2 tablespoonfuls of cornstarch dissolved in water, and boil till done, stirring constantly. Take off and let cool, then mix with the stiff-beaten whites of the eggs ; put in a dish to get cold ; turn out and serve with fruit juice. For 10 persons.

256. LEMON CREAM, No. 2.

¼ lb of sugar, yolks of 6 eggs, juice of 2 lemons, grated peel of one lemon ; beat all together ¾ of an hour ; add 1 oz. of gelatine soaked in a cupful of cold water ; put it in the dish it is to be served in and garnish with raspberry or any other kind of jelly This pudding may be made with milk and flavored with vanilla instead of lemon juice. For 10 persons.

257. CHOCOLATE CREAM, No. 1.

1 quart of sweet milk, ¼ lb. of unsweetened chocolate, vanilla to taste, 1 tablespoonful of cornstarch, ½ lb. of sugar.

Dissolve the chocolate in a little water over the fire and boil with the sugar, milk and vanilla. Meanwhile dissolve the cornstarch in a little of the milk or water. Keep the chocolate, milk and sugar still boiling on the stove and add slowly a few tablespoonfuls of it to the cornstarch and milk or water; then pour all together, stirring until it has thickened sufficiently. Take off and let it cool in a glass dish or china mold. Serve with vanilla wafers and vanilla sauce.

This is a very dainty and desirable desert when eggs are scarce.

258. CHOCOLATE CREAM, No. 2.

6 oz. sweet chocolate, 6 eggs, 4 oz. sugar, little vanilla and ½ oz. gelatine.

Melt the chocolate over the fire in a little water ; take off, and add to it while stirring, the sugar and vanilla, and then the yolks of the eggs ; beat all together well, put back on the fire and let cook till it comes to a boil ; then set aside and add the gelatine dissolved in water and the stiff-beaten whites of the eggs. Put it into a china dish wet with cold water. When ready to serve turn out and serve with beaten sweet cream.

259. CHOCOLATE CREAM, No. 3.

Melt 3½ oz. of chocolate on the fire with 1 quart

of milk, add yolks of 6 eggs and stir over the fire till thick ; then beat well ½ pint of cream and mix it with the above. Melt 3 oz. of gelatine with water on a moderate fire, put through a hair sieve and mix with the whole. This is to be set aside to cool and stiffen either in cups or a form as preferred. Serve with vanilla wafers.

260. CREAM WITH ALMONDS.

1 pint of good fresh cream, 2 oz. of finely grated almonds, ½ lb. sugar.

Cook all 15 minutes and let cool ; then beat 4 eggs, and the yolks of 3 eggs into it. Pour this mixture into custard cups and set them in hot water to thicken. Serve hot or cold. If to be served cold set on ice.

261. CREAM WITH FRUIT AND JELLY.

Take sweet or sour cream, the first creams quicker, and beat to a foam ; mix with it sugar, sliced cooked or canned fruit.

262. TUTTI-FRUTTI, No. 1.

Cover the bottom of a large glass dish with macaroons and lady fingers ; pour over this fruit juice and white wine to taste, and let soak an hour. Meanwhile let come to a boil 1 tableapoonful of butter, to which add 3 pints of milk and the yolks of 5 large eggs ; add sugar and vanilla to taste ; stir till thick but do not let it come to a boil ; take off, let it cool and pour over the cakes in the dish. Beat the whites of the eggs stiff, sweeten with sugar and fruit jelly and spread on top.

263. TUTTI-FRUTTI, No. 2.

Cover the bottom of a glass dish with cakes as in No. 1 ; over these lay finely-cut fruits or jelly in lumps.

Make the same mixture to pour over them except that the stiff-beaten whites are to be stirred in it instead of being spread on top.

264. CREAM OF CORNSTARCH, No. 1.

1 quart of milk, 2½ oz. of sugar, 3 eggs, 1 table-spoonful of cornstarch, a little rose water to tasae.

Put ½ of the milk with the sugar on the fire ; stir into the other half of the milk the yolks of the eggs and the cornstarch (dissolved) and pour this into the boiling milk and let it boil for some time together ; take off, add the rose water (only a few drops), and put in the glass dish to serve. Garnish with pieces of jelly.

265. CREAM OF CORNSTARCH, No. 2.

1⅛ quarts of water, ¼ lb. sugar, ¼ lb. cornstarch or corn meal, juice of 3 lemons and grated peel of 1 lemon.

Let the lemon juice, peel, sugar and ½ of the water come to a boil. Mix the cornstarch in the other half of the water and add to the other ingredients ; boil for 10 minutes. Serve with any kind of fruit sauce.

266. ORANGE CREAM.

Beat 1 quart of sweet cream, juice of 6 to 8 oranges and ½ lb. of sugar. Beat all together well, add then 1 oz. of dissolved gelatine and serve in a glass dish.

267. GOOSEBERRY DISH.

1 quart of green gooseberries, cleaned and washed ; boil them with 1 quart of water till done ; stir through a sieve and sweeten. Put on the fire and stir into it ½ lb. of rice flour which is mixed with the gooseberry juice. Let it boil for a while, stirring all

the time, then pour into a dish wet with cold water, and serve with sweet cream.

268. SAGO PUDDING.

Soak ¼ lb. sago in hot water ; pour off the water and add ½ pint of raspberry and ½ pint of currant juice, with sugar and lemon juice to taste ; boil till stiff, being careful not to let it burn. Serve with cream or milk.

269. STRAWBERRY CREAM.

2 lbs. ripe strawberries, ½ lb. of sugar, whites of 6 eggs, 1 glass of cider or red wine.

Wash the berries well, pour water off of them, then stir through a sieve. Boil the wine with the sugar ; add the fruit and a tablespoonful of cornstarch ; stir frequently till it comes to a boil again; take off, beat the whites stiff and stir into the fruit. Serve or garnish with fine ripe strawberries.

270. FRUIT DISH.

Cut 2 bananas in fine lengthwise slices and lay them in a glass dish, upon this a layer of ½ of a ripe pineapple cut in small pieces, and then a layer of sliced oranges; pour sugar and a little water over and continue these layers of bananas, oranges and pineapples till the dish is full. If canned pineapples is used take the pineapple juice instead of water. Put on ice. A delicious dessert for hot days.

271. RASPBERRY FOAM.

Beat the whites of 5 eggs very stiff and stir into it 3 tablespoonfuls of raspberry jelly and ½ tablespoonful of sugar. Serve in glasses.

272. SOUR CREAM FOAM.

Beat the whites of fresh eggs very stiff; to each egg allow 1 tablespoonful of thick sour cream ;

sweeten, and flavor to taste with grated lemon peel
or vanilla. Beat the cream till light before adding
to the stiff whites. Serve in glasses.

273. FLAMMERY WITHOUT EGGS.

¼ lb. cornstarch, 3 oz. grated blanched almonds, 3
oz. of sugar, grated peel of ½ lemon and a little
vanilla.

Stir well all together with 1 pint of milk and
add to it 3 pints of boiling milk. Let boil while stirring till it separates from the pan. Take off, let cool
in a glass dish and serve with fruit jelly or fruit juice.

274. APPLE CREAM.

Cook 1 soup plate of sliced apples in plenty of sugar;
cover the bottom of a glass dish with them ; over
this put a layer of biscuit cakes 2 inches deep. Meanwhile let 1 quart of milk come to a boil with a little
vanilla, into which pour a tablespoonful of cornstarch
dissolved in a little milk ; boil, stirring all the while.
Finally add the well-beaten yolks of 3 eggs and pour
over the apples and biscuits. After it is cool add the
beaten whites and garnish with jelly.

275. VANILLA CREAM.

5 pints of milk, 6 eggs, 1 tablespoonful of cornstarch, sugar to taste and a little vanilla.

Beat all together in a clean cooking vessel over
the fire till just before it comes to a boil ; take off, beat
a little longer and put in a glass dish. Serve with
fruit juice.

276. RUSSIAN CREAM.

1 bottle of good white wine, ½ lb. sugar, grated
peel of 1 lemon, juice of 2 or 3 lemons, 8 eggs, 1 tablespoonful of best cornstarch dissolved in water ; beat
all together well in an enameled pot on the fire till just
before it comes to a boil ; take off and stir till cool.

277. EGG CHEESE.

Beat 5 or 6 eggs thoroughly; while stirring add 1 quart of sweet milk, sugar to taste, and a few drops of rose water. Put in a deep pan, set in boiling water and boil till stiff. Serve with a sauce of vanilla, sugar and sour cream. Instead of being boiled, it may be baked in an oven and served with cold fruit juice.

278. SWISS CHEESE.

Beat the yolks of 5 eggs, 4 or 5 tablespoonfuls of sugar, the juice of 4 lemons and 1 quart of whipped cream together thoroughly. Put on ice and serve cold.

279. NOODLE CREAM.

Let 5 cups of milk with 3 oz. of sugar and the grated peel of 1 lemon come to a boil; put into this 3 oz. of fine noodles and let boil 10 or 12 minutes; then add the yolks of 5 eggs which have been beaten in a little milk. When cool add the whites of the eggs beaten stiff and the juice of 1 lemon. Serve with whipped cream or fruit juice.

280. LEMON JELLY.

Take 3 pints of water and the juice of 6 or 8 lemons, 5 oz. of sugar, 2 tablespoonfuls of cornstarch or best flour dissolved in a little of the water ; yolks of 6 eggs well-beaten, the grated peel of 1 lemon ; boil all together till stiff ; take off and when done add the whites of the eggs beaten stiff, and serve with sweet milk and sweet crackers or garnished with fruit jelly.

Instead of 6 or 8 lemons take ½ bottle of whlte wine and the juice of 2 lemons.

In case one does not wish to use the wine and the 6 or 8 lemons, these may be omitted, using all the

other ingredients and finally mixing in 3 tablespoonfuls of currant or raspberry jelly, to give a pretty
color and taste.

281. CREAM WITH BREAD.

Beat thick sweet cream to a foam. Grate some
rye bread and mix it with sugar and jelly to taste.
Serve the bread and cream in layers in a glass dish.

282. FRUIT JELLY.

Bring 1 quart of water to a boil, add 1 cup of
sugar, the juice of 6 or 8 lemons, and the same amount
of raspberry or other jelly ; mix 3 or 4 tablespoonfuls
of cornstarch with 1 cup of water and pour into the
above while boiling and stir till stiff; take off, put in a
glass dish to cool, then set on ice to harden and serve
cold with lady fingers.

283. PUEKLER ICE CREAM.

Whip cream till it is stiff, and sweeten as for ice
cream. Divide this in thirds ; flavor the first third
with vanilla ; the second color pink with raspberry
juice and the last third color with chocolate, first having dissolved the chocolate in a very little milk. Mix
into each part a few macaroons.

Put in an ice cream freezer in layers, do not turn
nor stir ; let it stand a day or longer, as necessary to
freeze, keeping covered with ice.

CAKES AND TARTS.

284. SAND CAKE, No. 1.

Beat 1 lb. of butter to a cream, add bye and bye
1 lb. of sugar, stirring all the time, yolks of 9 eggs
and 1 lb. of cornstarch.

Beat all together for an hour, then mix it with the juice of 1 or 2 lemons, vanilla to taste and the whites of the eggs beaten stiff; bake 1 hour in a cake pan.

285. SPECULATIUS CAKE.

1 lb. of flour, a scant lb. of sugar, ½ lb. of butter, the grated peel of 1 lemon, 3 eggs and a little cinnamon. Work these ingredients together quickly in a pan ; then put it in the ice box for 24 hours, after which work it a little, roll out thin, cut out with little cake cutters and bake in a moderate oven till light brown.

Before rolling out baking powder the size of a pea may be worked into the dough.

286. GERMAN CAKE.

Stew 2½ oz. Graham bread with a little butter for 2 minutes, then soak it with thin fruit or lemon juice ; beat the yolks of 10 eggs thoroughly with ½ lb. of sugar, grate 6 oz. of almonds with the peel and mix all together well ; finally add the whites beaten stiff. Bake in a quick oven.

287. MACAROONS.

Beat the whites of 8 eggs till stiff; mix into this 1¾ lbs. of sugar, 1 lb. chopped almonds, and the juice of 1 lemon. Drop by spoonfuls on a pan greased with butter or waxed ; bake in a moderate oven a while till a light brown.

288. PLUM CAKE.

Cream ½ lb. of butter, then beat for ½ hour longer with the yolks of 8 eggs; add ½ lb. of sugar, ½ lb. washed and cleaned seedless raisins, grated peel of 1 lemon, ½ lb. best flour, and finally the whites of 5 eggs beaten stiff. Bake 2 or 3 hours in a well greased pan in a moderate oven.

289 CORN CAKE.

Beat the yolks of 8 eggs and ¾ lb. sugar for ½ hour, add ½ lb. cornmeal, grated peel and juice of 1 lemon, 23 or 30 grated almonds and finally the whites of the eggs beaten stiff. Bake slowly 45 minutes.

290. CHERRY CAKE.

¼ lb. butter, ¼ lb. flour, 3 oz. sugar, 3 or 4 yolks of eggs and grated peel of 1 lemon.

Beat all together well and add the whites of the eggs beaten stiff. Put ½ of this mixture in a well greased pan, cover over this stoned cherries, and then pour over these the other ½ of the mixture, and bake slowly.

291. APPLE CAKE.

2 oz. of butter, yolks of 4 eggs, 5 oz. sugar.

Cream all together, add 6 oz. of best flour, and the whites of the eggs beaten stiff. Cover with thin sliced apples and bake.

292. SAND CAKE, No. 2.

Cream 1 lb. of butter well, to which add 1 lb. of sugar, yolks of 8 eggs and 1 lb. cornstarch. Beat all together well for 1 hour, then add the whites, the juice of 1½ lemons and vanilla to taste. Bake for 1 hour.

293. ALMOND CAKE.

Beat well 8 yolks of eggs with ¾ lb., of sugar add 4½ oz. of grated sweet almonds, 1 oz. of bitter almonds, ½ lb. of best flour and a little lemon juice. Mix all together well and add finally the whites of the eggs beaten stiff, and bake in a quick oven.

294. BREAD CAKE.

Beat the yolks of 12 eggs for ½ hour with ¾ lb. of sugar, 3 oz. of grated sweet chocolate, grated peel of

'₂ lemon or a little vanilla ; then add ³₄ lb. of grated stale bread, rye or graham, and mix all together with the whites of the eggs beaten stiff and bake. This cake may be covered with a coating of sugar melted in lemon juice.

295. RICE CAKE.

Wash 3 or 4 time ½ lb. of best rice ; boil in cold water till soft ; bring to a boil the juice of 6 lemons with 1 lb. of sugar ; put the rice into this and boil till dry ; take off and let cool ; add the peel of 3 or 4 lemons cut in pieces and boil till done. Put all in a well-greased pan or dish and bake for 1 hour. Serve and garnish with jelly.

296. NUT PUDDING.

Beat the yolks of 10 eggs with ½ lb. sugar ; add ¼ lb. grated peanuts, ¼ lb. grated almonds, juice and grated peel of ½ lemon, little vanilla, 2 oz. of best flour and finally the whites of the eggs beaten stiff. Mix all together well and bake in a moderate oven.

DRINKS.

297. CARAMEL CEREAL COFFEE.

Take 2 large cups of this coffee and 10 cups of cold water ; bring to a boil for 15 minutes.

298. DR. LAHMANN'S NAEHRSALZ COCOA.

Take for each cup of water 1 teaspoonful of cocoa, 1 teaspoonful of sugar and 1 teaspoonful of cornstarch for every 5 cups.

299. SOUR MILK.

Put fresh milk into a stone pot, let stand for 1 or 2 days in a room at about 60°. The skin on top must be light yellow and shiny ; before serving stir in cream with the milk well. Put on ice in summer and serve in glasses.

300. RASPBERRY LEMONADE.

2 quarts of water mixed well with 2 tablespoonfuls of raspberry juice.

301. LEMONADE.

Take juice of 1 lemon, add 2 tablespoonfuls of sugar and 2 cups of water.

Dr. Lahmann's Naehrsalz-Cocoa and Naehrsalz

For sale at the Quisisana Nature-cure Sanitarium, Cocoa, per lb., $1.25 ; Naehrsalz, small pots, $1.

Professor Tyrrell's J. B. L. Cascade,

The most perfect irrigating apparatus on the market, $6.00; with attachment for women, $7.00. For sale at the Quisisana Nature-cure Sanitarium.

Deimel Linen-Mesh Underwear. ❧

Pure linen ought to be worn next the skin, and the open woven Linen-Mesh is the healthiest underwear ever made.   For sale at the

Quisisana Sanitarium,   Asheville, N. C.

The Prescott-Stanyan Bread Mixer and Kneader.

This machine not only produces better bread, but saves time and labor to a greater extent than any other kitchen utinsil used; even the wringer not excepted.   For sale at the Quisisana Sanitarium, Asheville, N. C.

Kneipp Health Store Co.

111 E. 59th STREET,
NEW YORK, N. Y.

Sole agents for Father Kneipp's only genuine Herb Remedies, put up by the only authorized firm, Oberhauser & Landauer, Wuerzburg, Germany.

Also a complete stock of Kneipp's books, herbs, health food, such as malt coffee, whole wheat bread, strength giving soup-meals, the celebrated Kraft-Suppe, Kern-Lentils, peas, oats, barley, Grunkern soup, etc. Dr. Lahmann's and Bilz's nutritive-health cocoa, vegetable milk extract and biscuits. Specialties for vegatarians, grape juice, German unfermented wine, etc. Kneipp's & Dr. Walser's Aircell Health Underwear in Chinagrass, Linen, Tricot, and Cotton ; Sandals, ventilated Shoes, water cure appliances, such as steam baths, packs, massage rollers, etc. Write for free illustrated and descriptive catalogue and "Guide to Health."

PUBLICATIONS ON NATURAL METHODS:

Kneipp Water-cure Monthly . . . . $1.00 per year
American Kneipp-Blaetter . . . . $1.00 "   "
B. Lust Gesnudheits Calendar . . . . .25 "   "

B. Lust, Publisher and Editor. Director of the Kneipp Institute, 111 E. 59th street, New York, and of Kneipp Sanitarium "Bellevue", Butler, N. J.

Sample copies of Kneipp monthlies mailed free to those mentioning "Quisisana Hygienic Cook Book."

www.ingramcontent.com/pod-product-compliance
Lightning Source LLC
Chambersburg PA
CBHW021416090426

42742CB00009B/1164